Funny and Inspiring Stories From Around the World

Funny and Inspiring Stories From Around the World

Edited by
Keith Danby

Authentic

Copyright © 2004 Keith Danby

10 09 08 07 06 05 04   7 6 5 4 3 2 1

First published in 2004 by Authentic Media
9 Holdom Avenue, Bletchley, Milton Keynes, MK1 1QR, and PO
Box 1047, Waynesboro, GA 30830-2047, USA
www.authenticmedia.co.uk

British Library Cataloguing in Publication Data
A catalogue record for this book is available from the British
Library

ISBN 1-85078-603-8

Unless otherwise stated Scripture quotations are taken from the
HOLY BIBLE, NEW INTERNATIONAL VERSION.
Copyright © 1973, 1978, 1984 by the International Bible Society.
Used by permission of Hodder and Stoughton Limited. All
rights reserved. 'NIV' is a registered trademark of the
International Bible Society. UK trademark number 1448790

Excerpts from Philip Yancey taken from **Rumors of Another
World** by PHILIP D. YANCEY. Copyright © 2003 by SCCT.
Used by permission of The Zondervan Corporation.
Excerpts from John Ortberg taken from **If You Want to Walk on
Water, You've Got to Get out of the Boat** by JOHN ORTBERG.
Used by permission of The Zondervan Corporation.

Cover design by STL Design and Production
Illustrations by Anna Danby
Print Management by Adare Carwin
Printed and bound by AIT Nørhaven A/S, Denmark

Contents

Contents

Clean me up

by Philip Yancey

Once a week or so, my church schedules a 'Mom's Night Out' with free babysitting for single mothers who need a night off or mothers who simply want to spend an evening with their husbands. Our pastor's wife once happily took advantage of this programme to go out to dinner with her husband. Later, when Peter, my pastor, went to pick up his three-year old son, the babysitter told him about one of the games they had played. She had asked each of the preschoolers what was Mummy's favourite thing to do with them. 'You know what your son answered? He said that Mummy's favourite thing was to "clean me up."'

'In truth,' said Peter the next Sunday, 'that isn't Susan's favourite thing to do with her son. Cleaning him up is an excuse to hold him. Absorbing the mess is just part of the process of getting close. And it's the same with God.'

Facing Up to Poverty: India

by Stephen Rand

It was only a small slum. As before, it was squeezed on to a piece of wasteland between relatively grand apartment buildings. It didn't seem much bigger than a football pitch, yet it had been home to around 300 families, crowded close together in their rough, makeshift dwellings. It was a disaster waiting to happen. Apparently one family had been using a paraffin stove. It had tipped over, and set their home on fire. In minutes it had spread to the whole slum, moving through the tightly packed houses with great ease and frightening rapidity. In minutes it was all over; the poor do not have much to burn.

That was what I heard. All I saw was a blackened piece of waste-ground. In the middle, a solitary figure, crouched and huddled, clutching a stick with which he raked desultorily, almost absent-mindedly, through the ashes. He and his family had lived here for years. Every day he went out to collect empty and discarded jute sacks. Any he found he washed, then resold. Most days he made enough from this basic recycling to keep his family going. He began to build up his stock. With no storeroom, no room for expansion, he kept his stock on the floor of his home. The whole family lived on their reserves, their savings. All their worldly wealth formed their foundation and their carpet.

The fire had taken it all. Years of work lost in minutes. He crouched in the ashes, enveloped in an invisible haze of grief and despair. I stood in silence, then felt anger welling up inside me. The rage from my student days re-awoke. I wanted to kick, to lash out, to hurt. But who? There was no focus, but there was anger. I was confused and slightly ashamed. It seemed an odd and for me a very unusual emotional reaction.

Years later, John Stott, Tearfund's President, came to speak at our weekly staff prayers. He chose the topic of 'motivation' and talked about how Jesus was motivated into action by his reaction to suffering, the result of sin. He talked about his compassion – but he also talked about the Greek word used in the New Testament to describe another dimension of his reaction: he 'snorted with indignation'. So when Jesus was faced with the despair and injustice of human suffering he reacted with anger. I remembered my own reaction that day in Madras, and I felt a tinge of comfort and hope.

'Poppie, I am Sorry. It was Theft'

by Peter Meadows

Her name was Poppie – a bright young girl helping the Ugandan family in whose humble village home I was a guest. She seemed to spend endless hours fetching water from the village borehole. And helping prepare food and cook it over a wood fire in an area between the cabbage patch and the back door.

But what caught my eye, even more than Poppie's bright smile and servant heart, was she did it all wearing a Ralph Lauren designer top. Something that would cost the serious side of £25 in the UK and be much prized by my kids. Of course, she had no idea of the riches on her back. So I told her and watched her bright eyes grow even wider.

To Poppie it was just another top bought with a few Ugandan shillings – the equivalent of UK small change. How this had happened was no mystery. African markets seem full of such items – dumped due to being last year's range or beyond their sell-by date. Which explains the proliferation of Elton John World Tour 1998 and Euro 2000 and the like incongruously adorning backs across the continent.

All well and good. But not for long. On the final day of my visit I looked up to see Poppie with a neatly folded bundle in her hands. It was her Ralph Lauren top. 'Please would you take this as a gift for your children?' she offered. And I was about to get it wrong – in spades.

Come on now. I was the one here to do good. To be the hero. To make the sacrifices. To extend my benevolent generosity. But I had been caught on the back foot. There was no script for this – and, forced to ad lib, I blew my lines.

'Oh Poppie, thank you. But no. You need it far more than they do. Thank you. But you keep it.' In my mind was the fact that my kids had 'everything' and it would take her weeks to scrape up even the few pence for a replacement. But I was so wrong, wrong, wrong! Never have I seen a face move from beaming to crestfallen with such swiftness.

How long Poppie had agonised about offering this sacrifice I can only imagine. But this was her way of showing gratitude for my somewhat meagre contribution to her community. It was her opportunity to be the hero – and I had stolen it from her. And there was no way back.

That simple incident will haunt me for ever. It is a challenge to all we may seek to do with those who are poor. How often do those who work among poor communities consign them to being passive 'grateful-or-else' recipients of our own self-promoting kindness? How little do we earnestly seek ways in which they can be the heroes?

How often do we steal from the Poppies of this world their opportunity to behave as though they are rich – with something to offer us?

'Poppie, I am sorry! Through your own act of selfless generosity you taught me one of life's greatest lessons. Something far more valuable than even your Ralph Lauren top. Thank you.'

Hot-air Balloon Ride

by John Ortberg

Some years ago my wife arranged for us to ride in a hot-air balloon as a birthday gift. We went to the field where the balloons ascended and got into a little basket with one other couple. We introduced ourselves and swapped vocational information. Then our pilot began the ascent. The day had just dawned – clear, crisp, cloudless. We could see the entire Canejo Valley, from craggy canyons to the Pacific Ocean. It was scenic, inspiring and majestic.

But I also experienced one emotion that I had not anticipated. Want to guess?

Fear.

I had always thought those baskets went about chest high, but this one only came up to our knees. One good lurch would be enough to throw someone over the side. So I held on with grim determination and white knuckles.

I looked over at my wife, who does not care for heights at all, and relaxed a bit, knowing there was someone in the basket more tense than I was. I could tell, because she would not move – at all. During part of our flight there was a horse ranch on the ground directly behind her. I pointed it out because she loves horses, and, without turning around or even pivoting her head, she simply rolled her eyes back as far as she could and said, 'Yes, it's beautiful.'

About this time I decided I'd like to get to know the kid who was flying this balloon. I realized that I could try to psyche myself up into believing everything would be fine, but the truth was we had placed our lives and destinies in the hands of the pilot. Everything depended on his character and competence.

I asked him what he did for a living and how he got started flying hot-air balloons. I was hoping for his former job to be one full of responsibilities – a neurosurgeon, perhaps, an astronaut who missed going into space.

I knew we were in trouble when his response to me began, 'Dude, it's like this . . .'

He did not even have a job! He mostly surfed.

He said the reason he got started flying hot-air balloons was that he had been driving around in his pick-up when he'd had too much to drink, crashed the truck and badly injured his brother. His brother still couldn't get around too well, so watching hot-air balloons gave him something to do.

'By the way,' he added, 'if things get a little choppy on the way down, don't be surprised.

I've never flown this particular balloon before, and I'm not sure how it's going to handle the descent.'

My wife looked over at me and said, 'You mean to tell me we are a thousand feet up in the air with an unemployed surfer who started flying hot-air balloons because he got drunk, crashed a pick-up, injured his brother, and has never been in this one before and doesn't know how to bring it down?'

Then the wife of the other couple looked at me and spoke – the only words either of them were to utter throughout the entire flight.

You're a pastor. Do something religious.

So I took an offering.

First Ever Flight to India: February 1988

by Keith Danby

I remember well my first ever flight to India. I had only been with Send the Light Limited for six months and I could not describe myself then as an experienced traveller. I had only ever done the 'package holiday' travelling. It was understood that soon after taking up the position of Chief Executive of STL, I would have to visit India to meet the OM India leaders, and see first hand some of the things OM India was involved in.

This was a terrifying experience for me. As someone who does not enjoy spicy cuisine, can smell an Indian curry at five miles and having never been on a long-haul flight, it was all new to me. I lived in Bromley at the time, and I was due to take an Air India flight from London Heathrow to Bombay at 9:30 a.m. Although I had my visa, and had been taking my malaria tablets for a week, I still had not received the ticket. I got a call from the OM travel office in Carlisle to say that I was to collect my ticket from the Air India travel desk at Terminal 3 at Heathrow and, therefore, should be there in good time. I got up in what seemed like the middle of the night, travelled by car to the airport, and arrived far too early, just before 6.00 a.m., three-and-a-half hours before the flight. Little did I know that this was to be an eventful day!

At any time of day, an international airport like Heathrow is a busy place and, even at 6.00 a.m., the terminal was a hive of activity: except for the Air India travel desk, which was all closed up, when I eventually found it. I waited around, fearing the worst, and just after 7.00 a.m. an Indian lady, beautifully dressed in her Air India sari, opened up shop. By this time I was one of several people waiting to make enquiries. I was the first in the queue. I told my story, gave her the locator number I had been told to quote, and thought it would be a simple task to collect the ticket.

It did not take me long to realise that I had a problem. The agent looked through the various files, drawers and passenger lists she had but could not trace anything that linked the locator number or my name. She told me very politely that she could not issue the ticket as she had no authorisation telex from the travel agent. Fortunately, I had the home telephone number of my OM colleague, so I beat a hasty path to the nearest telephone to call him at home, even though it was only 7.30 a.m. He was puzzled but said he would call the agent in Manchester whom he had booked the ticket through; fortunately he had his home number. I was to call back in thirty minutes. I went back to the Air India desk to assure the agent I was on the case, but would need to wait until 8.00 a.m. to call for some information.

At 8.00 a.m., I promptly called back to be told that the Manchester travel agent had already left his home and was on his way to his office in downtown Manchester. My friend would keep trying. Once he had contacted the Manchester agent, he would get him to call or telex the details through to the Air India desk. I was told to go back and wait for this to happen and not to worry: it would be sorted. At this stage, I was beginning to feel agitated, but tried to keep my cool. When I arrived back at the Air India desk, I found a man who was not keeping his cool and was very agitated. Clearly very unhappy, he was shouting abuse at the poor Air India lady. I realised that perhaps this sort of thing happens every day at airports around the world.

I waited patiently, feeling increasingly sorry for the unhappy Air India ticketing agent, who was having to face this fierce onslaught from the man who wanted to be on the same flight as me. She stood firm and, although calm, remained insistent that there was nothing she could do to help him. She then turned to me to try sort out my problem. I remained friendly and polite and knew very well that my difficulty was not of her making. By this time, it was almost 8.30 a.m. She advised me that I should take my bags and have them checked through the security screen, just in case. I came back and at 8.45 a.m. she asked one of her colleagues to take me to the check-in desk and get a seat allocation, just in case. At just before 9.00 a.m., an excited agent came to me to say that the Manchester travel agent had sent a telex and now my ticket could be issued. I rushed across to get my ticket with a huge sense of relief. I was handed the ticket, exchanged warm thanks but there was no time to wait: I had to run to gate 53 where they were already boarding the aircraft.

It's in times like these that you realise just how big these airports are. Gate 53 was a fifteen minute walk away. As I ran into the departure lounge, which was by now almost empty with the last remaining passengers boarding, I was greeted by an official-looking gentleman in a smart uniform who said, 'Mr Danby?' I said 'Yes?' He said 'Would you mind waiting for a moment; we have been informed there is a problem with your ticket!'

A few moments later, the Air India ticketing agent, whom I had kept busy for the past two hours, ran into the lounge. She came straight to

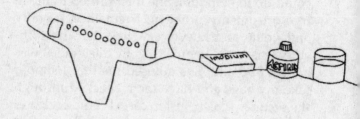

me and said 'Mr Danby, we think you have had enough trouble already today and we have upgraded you to business class!'

As I settled into the roomy leather seats, my head was pounding and I quickly looked in my carry-on bag for my large array of medical supplies. I was like a mobile pharmacist. I had been well briefed by experienced OM India travellers and I was stocked up with mosquito repellent, antiseptic cream for inspect bites, Imodium for Delhi belly, water purification tablets, soluble headache tablets, non-soluble headache tablets, emergency first-aid kit; the lot! I needed a headache tablet. I asked for a glass of water and in haste took two tablets. Thirty minutes later, puzzled as to why I was not feeling any better, I realised I had taken two water purification tablets for my headache!

As we reached our cruising altitude, I began to settle back and enjoy the delights of business-class travel. I could not believe how God had taken care of me and provided for me so well. I read a Psalm and prayed for a few moments to express my thanks and to commit the rest of the journey to the Lord. As I lifted my head and opened my eyes, I was shocked to see the passenger next to me, whom I hadn't really noticed, leaning over and looking at my open Bible, resting on my lap.

He immediately asked me if I was a Christian. For the rest of the journey we chatted and exchanged the details of what we both did for a living. He was a senior executive in the oil industry, based in the USA with business interests in India. He made the journey from Detroit to Delhi once a month. He went on to tell me that for the last three nights he had not slept well, because he had been invited to see a Christian dramatisation of the crucifixion. He could not forget the images of Jesus dying on the cross for what he was told was his sin. He asked if I could explain to him more about my faith. For several hours we talked and studied the scriptures together. In a simple childlike way, we prayed together and he committed his life to be a follower of Jesus.

What appeared to be administrative incompetence at 7.30 a.m. that morning, several hours later from 33,000 feet in the air, looked like the divine act of a sovereign God!

The Extra Mile

by Jeff Lucas

The late afternoon sun was wonderfully warm on our backs as we filed through the turnstiles, our day at Colorado's *Water World* at an end, or so we thought. We'd screamed, slid and splashed our way down dozens of chutes and raft rides, and now our bodies ached with the pleasant feeling of tiredness that tops off a good day of fun.

We picked our way through the hundred of cars. Our vehicle was easy to spot, loaded down as it was with all our bags and suitcases. This was an extended trip and although our car had no kitchen sink within it, we did seem to have a lot of stuff. As we approached the car, my feeling of sleepy peace was suddenly shattered, as was the driver's window of our car. We had been robbed. Out of a sea of hundreds, perhaps thousands of cars, ours had been selected. Glass littered the concrete. My heart sank like lead.

Tearfully, frantically, we checked our bags to see what had been stolen. Most things were intact. A laptop computer, which I had foolishly left sitting on the back seat had been ignored: perhaps the thieves had been disturbed and had beat a hasty retreat. But there was a crucial item missing: a bag that contained Kay's jewellery, together with our passports, and the valuable resident alien cards (called green cards, even though they're blue) that are proof that we are entitled to live in America. Our airline tickets were gone too. Obviously, without passports, we would not be able to return to the UK. We would have to fly to Los Angeles to the British Embassy there to get them replaced, and then on to Portland, Oregon to get replacement alien cards at the American Immigration Building. All of this would have to be done in the next day or two, and would cost us thousands in airfares. We were devastated.

Kelly stamped around the car park, hoping that maybe she would find that the passports had been discarded by the fleeing robbers, without success. Richard got on the phone to the police, and Kay wept with frustration: this was going to totally destroy our holiday. And for one rare moment in my life, I didn't panic, but felt a rush of inspiration and faith. Understand, dear reader, this is a rarity for me. Kay usually has the responsibility to be calm in a crisis and filled with faith. In the partnership that is ours, I usually accept the role of panic-stricken, uptight and agitated reactor, a role that I play with ease – it comes very naturally to me. But on this occasion – loath as I am to admit it in case you think me smug – I didn't feel panic at all, but sensed that all was going to be well. I gathered the family around and made an announcement that must have seemed like insanity.

'I think that we're going to get this stuff back in the next twenty-four hours', I announced, the wildness of the statement beginning to dawn on me even as it came out of my mouth. 'Let's ask God to help us – he can do it.'

I don't know if it was just wishful thinking, or a genuine gift of faith, but I said it anyway, and, right there in the car park, our feet crunching on the broken glass, we put our request in to God. 'Please get our stuff back.'

The police arrived, took our details, and told us that hell was likely to freeze over before we got our stuff back. Passports were very saleable, and anyway, mused the officer, 'Those thieves will be miles away from here by now.' We were advised to plan a trip to the West Coast to replace the stolen documents – and be quick about it. We drove to our hotel, the wind blasting now through the shattered window. A quick call to the British Embassy, answered by an official who had a Masters degree in blatant unhelpfulness, confirmed our fears. We would, all four of us, have to make the journey. But we had prayed and so we decided not to allow the fun that had kissed the early part of the day to be stolen along with the passports. And we did have a wonderful evening together.

The next morning, we decided to go to the airport to report the loss of our tickets. The ticket clerk tapped away on her keyboard for a minute or two and then everything changed; the sun came out from behind the clouds as she spoke.

'I have good news for you. Your passports, alien cards and air tickets have been found. They were discovered in a bush by a passer-by yesterday. Here's his number – he's eager to meet you. Here, make the call now.'

Breathless with excitement, I called our Good Samaritan. Apparently, the thieves had dumped our document wallet some miles from the water park – in that, at least, the policeman had been right. The wallet could have lain at the side of a road or under a bush for years, or perhaps never have been discovered. But this knight in shining armour of ours had seen something sticking out under the bush at the back of his home and, realising just how important these documents were, he immediately went to work. He called the police to report the find, who casually told him that they would stop by in the next few days to pick the wallet up; they did not connect our reported loss with his reported find at all. Impatient with that, he told the police not to bother – he would track us down himself. Finding a receipt from a hotel, he called there, only to be told that we had checked out days earlier. Undeterred, he called some friends of ours in Oregon – their card was in the wallet – but they had no idea where we were or how to contact us. He then realized that we were from England, found some UK phone numbers that we had written down and were in there too, and he began to systematically call these transatlantic numbers, in a desperate and diligent search to track us down. Finally, discovering the airline tickets, he called the airline and had them put a note into our computer reservation, so that when we checked in, we would receive the wonderful news. I drove across the city, thanking God all the way. We were to get everything back, except a couple of items of jewellery, within twenty-four hours.

But we did so because one man – who I don't think was a Christian – went the extra mile. He greeted us like long lost friends. We bought him dinner, a somewhat feeble attempt to express our thanks for the timely rescue operation that he had mounted. He didn't know us from a bar of soap, but had simply decided to go out of his way to be kind. As we parted with handshakes and hugs, we thanked God for answering our prayers – and doing so through a stranger's decision.

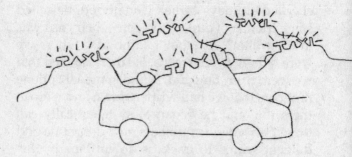

Entering Another World:
January 1980

by Stephen Rand

Nothing had, or perhaps could have, prepared me for the impact of my first minutes of experience of the Third World. I stepped through the door of the arrivals hall into another world. The first thing that hit me was the heat. It was now about midnight, it was January, it was dark . . . and it was hot. I think the hall must have been air-conditioned, because it was like stepping out into an open-air sauna. It seemed unnatural.

And then there were the people. It was midnight, it was January, it was dark . . . and there were people everywhere. There were children,

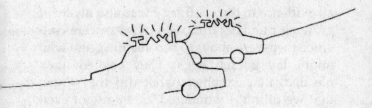

there were beggars, there were policemen, there were street-sellers, there were passengers who knew what they were doing, rushing off into the night. There were also the taxi-drivers. They spotted us. Their touts spotted us. We were potential customers.

Actually we weren't potential customers. Because Frank knew where we were staying and Frank knew the hotel had a courtesy bus. Frank knew that this bus would come to the point where we were standing and pick us up. He knew this even when the bus came towards us and then drove past, ignoring his vigorous signals. He knew this even when ten minutes later the bus came towards us again, and drove past us again, ignoring his even more vigorous signals. He kept to his beliefs when another ten minutes passed, and so did another bus.

Impressed as I was by a man who keeps his faith in the face of discouragement, who perseveres in spite of hardship, who believes despite all evidence to the contrary, I was also aware of growing numbers of taxi touts who were convinced we were about to become the geese who might lay golden eggs. They cajoled, they pleaded, they laughed (what did they know that we didn't, I wondered?) they might even have threatened. I certainly felt threatened.

I felt threatened because of the uncertainty, the unfamiliarity. I just did not know what to do next. I was not in control. It was dark, it was hot, it was noisy. I was the odd one out. It was not my world. It was exciting, yes, but slightly scary. Everyone else knew what was going on, but I did not. I had stepped into another world.

That's My Doughnut!

by J. John

There was a man at an airport, and he wanted to buy a bag of small doughnuts and a coffee. He bought his doughnuts and his coffee and was looking for somewhere to sit, but all the tables were taken. There was one table where there was just one man sitting, so he thinks, 'I'll go and sit opposite him.' He puts his coffee and bags down at the table, takes off his coat and sits in the chair. He takes the lid off the coffee cup and takes a sip. He picks up the bag of doughnuts and takes one out, and then puts the other doughnuts in the bag back on the table.

The second man sitting opposite him stretches over, picks up the bag of doughnuts, takes out a doughnut, starts eating it, puts the bag down and smiles. The other man can't believe it. 'I cannot believe he has just stolen one of my doughnuts,' he thinks. He is so amazed that he is dumbstruck and decides he had better not say anything, in case the man gets a bit violent.

Anyway, the first man picks up the bag, takes out another doughnut and moves it nearer to his coffee and as far away from the second man as he can. However, the second man then stretches over, picks up the bag of doughnuts and takes out another one and puts the bag back down on the table and smiles again. The first man just can't believe that the second man has just nicked two of his doughnuts. He thinks to himself 'What is the world coming to? Can you believe it!' He is really angry.

Anyway, the first man picks up the bag, takes out another doughnut, puts it again close to his coffee. The second man then gets up to leave. The first man, still sitting at the table, thinks 'It's about time you left, you doughnut thief!' The second man puts on his coat, picks up his bag and then stretches over and takes out the one last doughnut left in the bag, breaks it in half, puts half in his mouth, half on the bag, puts the bag on the table, smiles and waves and off he goes. The other man thinks 'I'm not going to touch that doughnut. I can't believe what the world is coming to.' Anyhow, he looks at his watch and he thinks, 'Oh, it's time for me to go too.' So he gets up, puts on his coat, bends down to pick up his bag and as he bends down to pick up his bag, sitting on top of his bag was his bag of doughnuts. The first man was complaining that the second man was stealing his doughnuts when, in fact, the second man was sharing his doughnuts.

Listen, God owns all the doughnuts, and not only does he own all the doughnuts, he owns the bag they are in, he owns the table they are sitting on, he owns the ground that the table is standing on. They are all God's doughnuts and we need to offer our time, our talents and our treasure to him to enrich the church and extend the kingdom.

Journey to Victory

by Sidney Muisyo

'To know God and to make him known. That is the gift that Compassion gave me that will make a difference for the rest of my life,' says twenty-four year old Harrison Mbugua from Kenya.

Harrison Mbugua runs a food kiosk, which he has named Victory Hotel, serving a menu of corn meal, chapatis, meat stew, samosas, tea, soft drinks and buns. His business is growing and he is planning to open another food kiosk soon.

When Harrison, the second child of a family of ten, was registered into Compassion's child development programme in 1990, he was in grade one with really no hope of ever going further academically. 'We were a large family, and given that my parents were poor, supporting all of us through school was not an easy task by any standards,' Harrison says.

At the AIC Thigio project, young Harrison found people that believed in him. They encouraged him to believe in himself and in a

loving heavenly Father who cared for his life.
'The project staff were truly amazing. I learnt
that despite my circumstances, I could be a success in life if I applied myself.'

Harrison continued with his primary education until grade eight. His results in the final
national grade eight examinations could not
allow him to continue with formal education
at secondary school. 'The social workers
encouraged me to still pursue my dreams of
supporting myself and my family. Since I had
been learning shoemaking at the project, I
decided to pursue the trade further. When the
time for my graduation from the Compassion-
assisted project arrived, I was not scared about
the future as I felt I could take care of myself
from there.'

During his graduation, the project gave him
a farewell gift of shoemaking tools. And with
that, Harrison set up shop in cobbling work. He
named his business Joy Shoe Repairs. 'Thinking
of how the Lord had been good to me through
Compassion, I had nothing but joy in my heart.
Besides, I liked to make my customers happy
whenever they came in for shoe-repairs.'

Within a short time, Harrison decided to try
his skills at another business. He started a small
food kiosk, which he named Hot Hot Hotel.
'Initially, I was just selling samosas and buns,
but soon, I was selling cooked food.' With the
capital he raised from Joy Shoe Repairs and Hot

Hot Hotel, Harrison felt confident that the food business was a better prospect. He had saved $103 and decided to look for another location and started Victory Hotel at Kawangware, at the outskirts of Nairobi city.

'I believe that with the Lord on my side, victory is assured in whatever I seek to do,' says a confident Harrison. The business grew and Harrison soon hired two workers to help him with the cooking and other errands around the food kiosk. 'Business has not been bad. I make an average of $9 a day and this is enough to sustain the business.'

At weekends, Harrison dons a different set of clothes and becomes an evangelist. He is a member of an evangelistic team known as Arise For Your Light Has Come. 'I really believe that without the Lord, I would be nowhere today. Life would not be worth living. That is why I like to tell people to arise and be freed from their chains by the Lord Jesus.'

The evangelistic team preaches all over the city of Nairobi, though it tends to focus on Kawangware, a densely populated slum area. Through the group's efforts, hundreds of people have been exposed to the gospel of Jesus Christ. 'Every day I remember to pray for my sponsor from the United Kingdom. Without his sponsorship, I would not be what I am today, let alone being an employer. I have never met him, but I truly thank the Lord for him and ask that he be blessed in everything he does. God bless him.'

Weekend Alarms and Excursions

by Adrian and Bridget Plass

Fever

A: All my darkest and most dreadful nightmares about being ill in a country far from home seemed to be coming true towards the end of our first week away.

It began early on the Thursday afternoon of that first week, the day when we returned from Tuital, with the sudden, stomach-lurching realisation that I was supposed to be writing and sending two articles to two different publications by tomorrow at the latest. Two! One would have been awful but just about feasible. Two! Being made as I am, my first response was to wilt like an unwatered lupin (an analogy drawn from bitter experience). The fact is that both Bridget and I were already wrestling with a shadowy fear that this whole bizarre Bangladesh exercise was some kind of cosmic test or exam that we were very unlikely to pass, even if they let us mark our own papers so that we could cheat. Why do I, in particular, always default to an assumption of failure? Much of my most vigorous activity is akin to that of a lazy child who rushes around feverishly cleaning up just before his parents return. I suppose that helps to explain my second response.

What could I do to make everything all right so that everyone in the world would still love me? Wandering out on to the balcony I gazed across the jumbled tops of houses towards the centre of the city, looking for inspiration. Something caught my eye. For one passing, puzzling moment I thought I was looking at a British-style cathedral in the far distance. I wasn't, of course. It turned out to be yet another building under construction, festooned with sacking, bristling with bamboo poles, the whole thing magically transfigured by a hazy shroud of smog. I sighed as I considered my lifelong love affair with cathedrals.

An idea struck me. One of those blessed articles was for a newspaper in Holland, the other for an English periodical. Dutch people were unlikely to read the English magazine, and only the Dutch ever actually learn Dutch, a language that requires its users to speak as if their mouths are full of Lego. Why should I not send the same piece of writing to both publications? Yes! Yes, I could do that!

Having borrowed a laptop computer, I sat down at the small table in our hotel room to

write a deeply considered, multicultural mas-
terpiece on my first impressions of Bangladesh.
I may well be wrong, for my personal history
offers a multitude of similar occasions to select
from, but I cannot recall ever feeling less like
writing a thousand words than I did on that
Thursday afternoon. Wise words from the
book of the prophet Nike, son of Adidas, sus-
tained me. 'Just do it.' Only my pride and my
fingers were willing, though. The other parts of
me clenched themselves and each other miserably, waiting for the job to be over and done
with.

As I saved my work and leaned the top of my
body wearily over the back of the chair, my
head was spinning and I seemed to be in the
grip of a slight fever.

Later, we set off along the noisy, darkening
streets to find somewhere to eat with our new
friend and guide, Sanjay Sojwal. Sanjay is
World Vision's senior communications officer
for the whole of Asia, and he had come to take
photographs, supervise the film crew that
would be arriving on Monday, and to take over
from Peter, who was due to fly back to the UK
that evening.

By now I was feeling quite ill and rather worried. Suppose, I thought, I were to become
really poorly for any length of time, what
would become of our trip and its purpose?
What on earth was God up to?

Sanjay turned out to be a highly intelligent and quite delightful companion, but it is impossible to escape the conclusion that, on that first evening, I must have presented to him as nothing more than a dull-witted *Coca-Cola* addict. For some obscure reason I ordered *two* bottles as soon as we took our seats, and then sat vacantly with my hand curled round one of them, finding a pathetic crumb of comfort in the coolly familiar, universal shape of the slimwaisted bottle. I ordered fish – grilled red mullet I think it was – but as soon as it arrived I wished from the bottom of my stomach that I hadn't. That red mullet may have been dead, but its spirit lived on. It was a large, fleshy fish, lying heavily on its side so that one huge, perfectly round eye was able to stare reproachfully up at me.

'There was a time,' quoth the eye dolefully, 'when I too believed that life had a meaning and a purpose, but now – well, as you can see, that time has passed. Tell me, what are *you* doing in Bangladesh?'

Hypnotised by the eye, I shook my head silently from side to side. I didn't know. I had no idea. Wiping my bedewed forehead with the back of one hand, and feeling a vague obligation to eat the dish that had been set before me, I used the other hand to poke the side of my fish with a fork. The eye seemed to widen to the size of a dartboard. I laid my cutlery down, knowing that there would be no point in picking it up again that evening. Suddenly I felt very sick and horribly dizzy and I desperately wanted to go home.

Illness that forces me to stay in bed does usually have one or two very positive aspects. It is the only time when I am able to abandon the fulfilment of my responsibilities, or perhaps more honestly, it's the only time when I'm able to abandon the drip-fed guilt caused by *not* fulfilling my responsibilities. Such a relief! It wasn't like that this time, though. Bridget and I had put an immense amount of emotional and organisational effort into our trip. Then there were World Vision workers in Great Britain as well as Bangladesh. They had gone to enormous lengths to make the project a success, however hazy the exact nature of that success might seem to us at the moment.

I lay awake for hours on that eternal Thursday night, streaming with perspiration, aching in every joint, my mind pumping out dismal images of the following day, when Bridget and I were scheduled to meet our sponsor child for the first time. We'd worried about false emotion. Huh! What a marvellously cosy luxury of a problem that was beginning to appear. Bridget would have to do it on her own now, and if this blasted illness persisted it was possible that I might never meet Shahnaj. Never meet her! What a nonsense that would make of the stupid book we were supposed to write when we got back. *If* we got back. *If* I survived. Really, when you thought about it, what was the point of it all? What was the point of anything, come to that? Nothing but randomness and falling kites and endlessly repeated negative patterns and dentists and disappointment and death playing the final hand . . .

Thus, raving and raging and sweating I crossed my particular desert towards the dawn, eventually collapsing into the centre of an inadequate but welcome little oasis of exhausted, uneasy sleep.

Poets

B: This morning, having slept very little, I wake with a splitting headache and a feeling of doom. Immediately I remember what it is. Today Adrian is due to lead a writers' workshop, but will he be able to? I somehow get him propped up in bed and will him to be better.

'Would you like to try getting out of bed just to see if maybe you feel a little better?' I say gently, but, I confess, with determined hopefulness.

Adrian pulls himself out of bed, stands up, sways and sits down heavily.

'I'm really sorry, Bridget,' he says in a rather unsteady voice, 'but I do feel horribly dizzy. I'm afraid I just can't do it.'

Even I have to admit in my heart that it would be difficult to facilitate a writers' workshop from a horizontal position, and that is the only position he is going to be able to adopt safely.

'I feel so dreadful,' he goes on, 'I know how important this is to Martin and now it's too late for him to let them know.'

It is indeed. I leave my sad specimen of manhood shivering dismally in bed and go into the other room where Adrian's briefcase bulges with all the trip information. I fish out the letter from Martin Adhikary, who bears the grand title of National Church Relations Co-ordinator, and, sitting on the plumpy red sofa, try to decide what to do.

Martin happens to be one of the most delightful people I have ever met, enthusiastic, warm and extremely energetic. He is also very committed to his job and has already told us how much he was hoping to encourage young Bangladeshi writers in this workshop. The letter before me is addressed to 'Respectable Christian Writers in Bangladesh' and invites them to meet 'our distinguished visitor' Mr Adrian Plass (a writer of great repute in Britain!!) who is to speak on 'the primary role and responsibilities of a Christian writer in a developing society in the new millenium'.

'Oh, no, he isn't,' I murmur to myself, 'I am. The respectable writers of Bangladesh are going to be addressed a) by a woman and b) by someone who has had one book published and is not in any shape or form a distinguished visitor. Poor Martin, poor writers.'

I deliberately block out any thoughts of having to cope with meeting Shahnaj on my own in the afternoon and go to have breakfast. At least, I discover myself thinking grimly, they can't serve me last today! My mood is not improved by the fact that I have been a mosquito banquet throughout the night and my face is covered in itchy red bumps.

Half way through my omelette I pull myself together. I haven't had to get up at six in the morning to share a latrine with countless others or join a queue to pump water to wash from a well several blocks from where I live. I haven't had to provide some sort of meal for six people living in a house smaller than our garden shed. I am not feeling sick or shivery like Adrian. And fortunately I do have a folder full of Adrian's stuff that I can read. Maybe if I just stick to reading stuff it will be okay. Then, surely, it will just be a case of suggesting a topic on which they can write, and all will be well. After all, they are described as young and inexperienced so they probably haven't ever attended a writing workshop before, so . . .

They turn out to be not all young, and they certainly are not inexperienced. As they stand one by one to introduce themselves I am quite overcome by how accomplished and experienced they are as writers, except for one who confesses to never having written anything at all and only being there to accompany his daughter who has.

'Ah yes,' comes a loud voice from across the room, 'but he was a freedom fighter.'

Cheers and applause follow this and I reflect yet again on the fact that in this young and passionate country those who fought for its independence are heroes of every situation they find themselves in, even a seminar for writers.

Now it is my turn and, apologising profusely for Adrian's absence I begin to describe the origins of his writing career and the link between his breakdown and consequent passion for communicating the love of God. It is into an atmosphere of sympathy and interest that I try to explain how Adrian has discovered that universal and deep truths can be communicated through simple family incidents. I share some of what we call the Katy stories, times when our daughter, especially when she was a little girl, said or did something which Adrian has been able to use to reflect our foolishness and God's love for his children. This seems to interest most of them, if nods and smiles are any indication, and it is with growing confidence that I turn to his poems. After all, I had been told there is a long tradition of poetry writing in Bangladesh, their most famous poet Tagore being held in high regard.

As I come to the end of one of my favourites, I sense something is not right. A dullness has crept into the atmosphere. They look disappointed. I choose another and this time, probably through desperation, I inject rather more passion into the reading than would be considered normal. They lean forward. At the end there is a murmur of appreciation. I begin again and this time give my rendition of *A Winter Waking* even more welly. Now I have them, and as I finish the last line, conscious that I am beginning to sound more like Edith Evans than Bridget Plass, there is a round of applause. Now it is their turn and as I set them the task of using an illustration from something closely familiar to life in Bangladesh to communicate a truth far more universal in application, I am relieved to see pens and notebooks in use. Having said that, there is also a good deal of loud conversation and I feel rather like an inadequate prefect in charge of detention! At last their time is up and I sit back, relieved that my part is over and Martin is now in charge.

'Now before we read what we have written,' says Martin smiling, 'are there any questions?'

Having fielded a fierce, 'Why are we sitting in a beautiful room reading poetry while our people starve?' and attempted a concise response to 'What is the difference between the

Christian writer and the non-Christian writer?',
Martin agrees that it is fine if they want to read
in Bangla and sits down.

As I listen to almost everyone reading in
their own language I realise why they were
disappointed by my earlier, tame readings,
and why they only responded enthusiastically
when I began to intone like Henry Irving.
Bangla is a tonal language, its rising and
falling inflections giving meaning and definition to each word. It is velvety and musical
with none of the hard edges of western
European languages. One by one the writers
rise to their feet and declaim their work with
passionate intensity. It is all very, very moving.
The only problem is that not only do I not have
a clue what they were talking about, but also I
don't know whether what they have written is
good, bad or utter rubbish! This doesn't matter, except that at the end of each one there is a
long pause, with yet another bright-faced,
expectant poet looking directly at me for a
response.

The situation is not entirely helped by Martin
occasionally leaning over and whispering
rather loudly, 'That one was very good.'

I smile and mumble and clap like a clock-
work clown until the last writer has finished,
but then comes one more question.

'In Bangladesh we Christian writers suffer
for what we write. We use our poetry to pierce

the armour of unjust government and Muslim domination. Why does Adrian not use his wit to attack your government's liberal attitudes to the growing power of the Muslim community in Britain?'

Just for one moment I feel really, really fed up with my husband for having the audacity to get ill, but then it is as if I sense that my reply matters to God. I try to lean back and hear what he would like me to say.

'In our country we find that if you attack too directly it can have the opposite effect to that which you want. People simply say "I don't have to read this rubbish" and they don't. What Adrian tries to do is to make people laugh and relax, then, while the critical side of their brain is not looking, slip in under the eye of their guard and attack the heart.'

It sounds rather good actually, and I see my husband's reputation growing before my very eyes. A sort of literary freedom fighter! I hope I haven't overdone it, aware that if I carry on like this I'll be in danger of creating a saint. I hurry on.

'The thing is, Adrian has been given the job of digging the ground ready for God to plant his seeds. For example, many men in our country don't feel the need to believe in God, so Adrian wrote this to try to stir them up.' I read, *When I Became a Christian* in my new dramatic style, only stumbling when I come to the line 'A quick salvation sandwich and a cup of sanctity'

– they'll never get that – and sit down utterly exhausted, but relieved that I have managed to get through my ordeal.

The moderator rises to his feet and, after thanking everyone for coming, explains that all are welcome to stay for cakes and – turning to me with a twinkle – a cup of sancti-tea!

Showered with the published works of the entire group and promising photocopies of all the poems I have read out, I remind myself of Adrian's favourite adage, 'All gigs pass', and try to prepare my mind for the afternoon visit to Hazaribagh slum.

The squalid conditions prevailing in the slums where more and more people from rural areas are taking shelter should be a matter of great concern to urban development planners. The planners must be aware of the fact that most of the slums pose a serious health hazard. They should take note of the ever worsening crime situation which has a lot to do with the slums and the ever growing ranks of unemployed youths. The task is not easy as the rural poor, pauperised by natural calamities and the absence of employment opportunities move to the urban areas in the hope of a better life. The vulnerability of these people is fully exploited by the urban touts and muscle men and many of them end up in the world of crime.

Dhaka Independent, Monday 17 January 2000

My Gift

B: The veil is about to be lifted.

We have driven through oldest Dhaka until the noisy, tacky glamour of the painted rickshaws and optimistic street traders has given way to increasingly narrow streets with tiny dirty shops, where flies, filth and open sewers create the rotting stench of decay. At last we bump to a halt in a small square outside what I am informed is the community centre, where Shahnaj and her friends will be waiting for me. The door opens and as we step into the dark interior, Joanna Rossario, who is in charge of the project, speaks.

'Do you recognise her?'

Everyone is smiling and I send up a prayer of prayers. 'Please let me recognise her from her last photo. Please, Lord, don't let me let her down:

There is no need whatsoever for me to worry. Standing in front of me is a group of children, clearly dressed up in their very best clothes. They are all beaming but only one of them has a lightbulb lit up inside her. Only one shines with a confidence I have rarely seen in any child. Her hair done up in delightful rag bunches, she dazzles me with her smile and then, just as I struggle with exactly how to greet this child who doesn't know me but who is joined in such a strange way to me and my family, she steps forward and proudly gives me a full-blown red rose. Then, with a gesture which instantly establishes that as far as she is concerned I am her possession, she takes my hand. I reach into my bag and awkwardly, one-handedly produce one of my small wrapped gifts, a set of hairbrushes. I give it to her expecting her to open it, worried that it might not be suitable. To my surprise, after thanking me she hands it unopened to the slightly older girl standing next to her. There is a pause. Some conversation takes place between Shahnaj and Joanna. I stand, smile fixed in place, feeling extremely large and rather foolish and wishing Adrian was with me.

There is a sudden flurry of activity. We are to go to her home. Right now. She is ready. She knows what to do. Steering me like some kind of farm animal on the end of a rope, she hauls me forward, pointing out the safest places to put my feet to avoid falling into the sewer, gesturing upwards to where the edges of rusty corrugated iron roofs threaten to slice open my head, dismissing with shrill authority those who gather in front of us, but who, in her opinion, have no part in her celebration, ordering a small boy who turns out to be her brother to run ahead, presumably to tell her mother we are on our way. And all the time she chatters. Lifting her face to mine with total joy she chatters without ceasing, clearly unaware that I can understand not one word of what she is saying.

I become aware of the other, older girl hurrying along with us. It is Shahnaj's sister, carrying my unwrapped present. Shyly she takes my other hand and, gaining confidence almost immediately, joins in the chattering.

I am completely entranced, if a little breathless. I begin to feel if we go much faster down these ever-narrowing alleyways we'll start to fly! Now we are so far ahead of the rest of the party that I can reasonably suggest we stop and wait, and I am amused to see the slight anxiety on the faces of the pursuing group as they round the corner and see that I have not been abducted by my small enthusiastic charges.

We make the last part of the journey in single file as the makeshift walls are now less than three feet apart. Dark, open doorways reveal glimpses of women and children but I can see nothing very clearly, determined as I am not to disgrace myself by arriving for tea with a foot covered in sewage! We have arrived. There are two steps leading to the doorway and I make a mental note of the fact that the house appears to be built on stilts. With Shahnaj in front and her sister behind I feel we are like the carriages of a toy train shunting into the station. It is dark and it is very, very small and seemingly full of shining white teeth. Standing in front of me is a tall thin man who shyly shakes my hand.

Almost the whole area is taken up with a double bed on which are perched two grinning boys, one the lad I've already met and the other an older teenager. Shahnaj and her sister, Simon, immediately scramble up on to the bed and urge me to join them, which I do. This is just as well, because by the time Sujit, Joanna and Peter join us there is about five inches spare standing space! A commotion at the door heralds the arrival of the woman of the house, her face alight, a baby in her arms. Now there are no inches at all and as a crowd of children have blocked the doorway it all bears a marked resemblance to what one imagines must have been the conditions in Noah's ark.

There is another grinning pause as everyone waits for me to do something. But what? I reach for my bag and hand out my gifts. Oh dear, I haven't really brought the right things at all. Whatever will Shahnaj's dad and older brother make of their box of Ferrero Rochers? Will her little brother, who seems to be about eight, be very disappointed with his notebook and pencils? Why, oh why didn't I check the ages of the family before coming? I give Simon and her mother selections of soaps and toiletries and thank God that I have brought brightly coloured books, one of which I give the baby 'for when she's older', and one to Shahnaj with a T-shirt we'd bought at Heathrow. I wait for them to open their presents or to show a response, but something is wrong. The smiles have faded. What have I done? An uncomfortable silence has fallen. Oh, my goodness, what have I done? Have I broken some law of protocol? Inadvertently insulted someone in the family? Then Shahnaj whispers to her mother, who holds up both her hands in a gesture of despair and says something to Joanna, who turns to me.

'They are very sad,' she says, 'because they have no gift for you.'

Somehow God gives me the right words. 'Seeing Shahnaj is my gift.' The smiles are back, breaking up the darkness like jewels in a cave. Now everyone is talking. They have forgotten all their questions. It is enough that I am here. They have waited so long. How many children have I? Four? My word, what happiness that seems to give them! The baby is pushed into my arms. I hope against hope that I can show how able I am as a mother. God obviously doesn't feel I deserve any more divine assistance. The baby howls! I hand her back ruefully to Shahnaj's mother. Snuffling and rubbing her dark eyes with a chubby hand the baby falls asleep. We smile at each other. No translation needed. I feel a newly familiar, skinny little hand creep into mine. Shahnaj shares our moment, putting her finger to her lips.

Suddenly it's time. Time to go. Right now. Another sudden decision is made with the jerkiness that I am getting used to. Now there is a ludicrous tangle of people occupying the three square feet of standing room. Much talking. Much reassurance that it is not a sad moment because we will be back on Sunday and Adrian will be with us (Oh, I do so hope so!). Much salaaming and handshaking and we are gone.

Along the alleyway, through the gathering crowd of children wearing an extraordinary assortment of dirty western clothes from frilly taffeta dresses to falling-to-pieces cotton knickers. Back to the office. Back to the van. Back finally to the hotel where a feverish, slightly wild-eyed Adrian asks me anxiously, what was it like?

'It was all right.' 'All right?'

Yes, all right. It was all right. I wasn't talking about the living conditions that I had glimpsed during the afternoon. Or the exhaustion I had seen etched into the face of the thin, shy man who was Shahnaj's father. Or the dirt, or the poverty. I was talking about something that had happened to me on my inner journey.

You see, that afternoon God had allowed the veil to be lifted – and it was all right.

The final gate

A: I did say that illness has one or two positive aspects for me, and at the risk of sounding loony to some readers and perfectly normal to others (I'm not at all sure which of those extremes bothers me most); I would like to offer you a second example of this.

Occasionally, and particularly in the case of a feverish illness, there has seemed to be a small, peaceful place right at the centre of the vortex, where I am able to hear God speaking more clearly than at any other time. Yes, of course it may be nothing but my imagination, but I hope it isn't, and I don't think it is. And that is what happened when I woke or didn't wake or half-woke from that short but blessedly welcome sleep of mine, the one that began in the early hours of Friday morning.

Dimly I registered the fact that Bridget had left to meet Shahnaj without me. And this – this must be me left here, I reflected crazily. Yes, this was me stretched out on the bed like a giant piece of damp asparagus, dozing and waking and dozing and waking. What on *earth* was going on? At one point I caught my swirling brain wondering if perhaps the fault lay with British Airways. God had somehow failed to arrive with our flight from England, just as all our luggage had failed to turn up in Australia ten years ago when we took our first major trip abroad with a different airline.

Then, quite abruptly, but with an odd, artificial clarity, I found myself in that hushed, unstirring place I mentioned before, a place where good health and sickness alike mean nothing.

In front of me stood one of those heavy, white, five-barred gates, the sort of thing you find on farm tracks and at the edges of fields all over Britain. Somehow I knew, with that unchallengeably certain knowledge peculiar to dreamlike episodes, that I would never be able to unlock this gate. Continuing along the path beneath my feet, one that for unrevealed reasons I was bound to follow, could only be accomplished by climbing to the other side. I was equally conscious, though, of being so hung about and weighted with bags and baggage of various kinds that, unless I abandoned at least part of my burden, the obstacle would be insurmountable. After a moment's pause, I let one of my bags fall to the path, clambered awkwardly to the top of the gate and dropped heavily to the ground on the other side.

I was made aware, without actually experiencing each occasion, that precisely the same thing happened with another five gates, each more difficult to negotiate than the one before, and each demanding that I discard more of my luggage. Then, as if I had reached the climactic scene in the sort of film that usually makes me cry, came the moment when I found myself standing in front of the seventh and last gate, a final hurdle separating me, as I now understood, from the place and the person that all followers of Jesus desperately hope to find at their journey's end.

One more gate

If I could simply haul myself up to the top and lower myself down on the far side, all my travelling would be done. One more gate, the highest and most difficult of all to climb – impossible to scale in fact, unless I surrendered my sole remaining item of luggage.

When I tell you that this final piece of impedimenta turned out to be my relationship with Jesus and the security that I felt in my closeness to him, you will understand why my heart nearly failed me. It was all I had left, and a small, frightened child's voice inside me cried out that if I just dumped this last and most precious possession of mine there would be no point in going on anyway. It was a nonsense. And yet, according to the inner voice of my dream, I had little choice. I could settle for an eternally unfinished journey, crouching here for ever on the wrong side of this gate hugging my imperfectly fashioned images to myself, or I could more or less joyfully embrace the risk, hoping and believing that Chesterton was right in defining paradox as 'The truth standing on its head'. I threw my last burden to the ground and began to climb . . . Probably just a dream, eh? But I would love to know if I made it or not.

'Y'all Ha' Grits?'

by Stuart Briscoe

I must confess that I boarded the British Airways 747 in London, at Heathrow airport, for my first trip to America with numerous misgivings. But there was one thing that gave me comfort. I knew that unlike many of the European countries I had visited, the natives spoke English. So I could, at least, communicate.

My first port of call was Chattanooga, Tennessee. I was met at the airport on arrival and transported immediately to a large, old hotel in the centre of town where I settle down for the night with a view to conquering jet lag. I failed, of course, woke up in the middle of the night and 'wished for the day'.

As soon as it arrived, I hurried to the restaurant and was greeted by an African American waitress who said to me, 'Y'all h' grits?' Assuming this was the standard greeting I replied 'Good morning.' She looked slightly bemused and repeated, 'Y'all h' grits?' Quickly gathering that the greeting had to be repeated, I dutifully responded, 'Good morning.' She looked around helplessly, called over a couple of other waitresses and they, after a hurried whispered consultation along with furtive looks in my direction, said – in formidable unison – 'Y'all ha' grits!'; working on the age old premise 'If they don't understand – shout!'

Recognising that we had a communication problem, I said sweetly, 'Does anyone here speak German by any chance?' I discovered to my dismay they spoke neither German nor recognisable English!

For the benefit of my non-American friends who would have been equally nonplussed by 'Y'all ha' grits?' let me explain. 'Grits' is – or are – (I am still not sure!) a kind of breakfast cereal that tastes only of whatever you put on it – or them! The young ladies were asking me 'Would you like some grits?' I was flummoxed by the 'y'all', as my mother had brought me up to believe I was singular, not plural, and the 'Ha' didn't add much to my comprehension either. Now if you've never heard of grits, have no knowledge of 'ha' and thought you were not a 'y'all', you too will have a problem in America.

So it was with exacerbated misgivings that I faced my first day in America. But worse was yet to come. The unknown driver whose job it was to transport me to the church startled me en route by leaning in my direction and saying, 'Would you like a chocolate kiss?' Having

learned from my early morning escapade with
the grits that it was incumbent upon me to go
with the linguistic, moral and ethical flow of
the new country, I hastily buried my British
reserve, puckered up and said, 'Sure, go ahead.
I don't care what it tastes like.'

And I was given a candy – a sweet that is!

Dying for a Drink

by Stephen Rand

We were introduced to Lily Chandrasekar. She was sitting on the low wall in front of the veranda of her simple dried-mud home. Next to her was a large framed black-and-white photograph of a man, black-haired and with a neat moustache. It was a photograph of her husband, and he was dead. At one point she propped the photo up on a chair, as if she wanted him to sit there once again. Lily told us the story. I asked an initial question; it was interpreted, and it was as if a tap of grief had been turned on. The story poured out. Lily did not wait for individual sentences to be translated. A torrent of words emerged with an intense passion, her eyes staring into the middle distance, focused on the past and not the present.

He had been the village school teacher, an active Christian – and also a harijan, a member of the low-caste community that made up less than a quarter of the village population of 3000. The water tank, the sole source for the village, was positioned in the high-caste, wealthier end of the village and many of them had piped connections to their homes. As a result, there was often little water available for the harijan community, the poorer people of the village.

Mr Chandrasekar had been one of the harijans who had taken their case to the local authorities, who had eventually decreed that the private water supplies to the high-caste Hindus should be disconnected and all water drawn equally from a tank in the centre of the village. It was to have ten taps: eight for the high-caste villagers, two for the harijans.

This was not a universally popular ruling and the tank became the focus of tension between the two communities, as the high-caste villagers objected to drawing water when the harijans were present. Six months before our visit the situation had come to a head, when the harijans were prevented from obtaining water at all. Lily's husband had gone to the high-caste village leaders to protest.

At this point, our interpreter explained, the story became confused. The police had intervened and arrested him, taking him to the police station. It was while he was being questioned that he had been beaten to death. Some claimed that high-caste villagers had taken the law into their own hands, killed him and then ensured there would be no backlash from the harijans by setting fire to forty-five of their houses and two school buildings.

As we listened to the story, and looked at the photograph, it seemed almost unreal. A Christian school teacher, about my age, beaten to death because of water. But Lily's face was real. She explained that every night her three year old, Noel, asked when Daddy would be coming home.

Do Not Despise the Small Things

by Keith Danby

It seemed a good idea at the time! I had taken a long weekend off and I was scheduled to be in the USA for three days. I was to fly on the Friday from Manchester to Chicago and meet up with my good friend, Dr Stephen Alfred, who ran the Bethany Hospital in Thane, India. It was Stephen's first time in America and the purpose of the trip was to raise awareness of the hospital and to get some prayer and practical support for the work.

From Chicago we would take a short flight to Grand Rapids. I knew Grand Rapids well as I visited there several times a year on business. There, we would be met by Ed Long, also a friend of long standing, whom I first met in England over twenty years earlier when we were both students at Capernwray Bible School. Ed now lived in Mount Pleasant, about fifty miles from Grand Rapids, and was a Professor at Central Michigan University. Ed had never met Stephen, but he had often heard me talk of him and the work of the hospital, and had agreed to arrange a breakfast on the Saturday morning for Stephen to talk about the hospital to a number of Christian leaders and business people.

I have to confess to being somewhat disappointed the next morning to discover that the breakfast was to be in Ed's home and that there would only be a handful of people. Four visitors, Ed and his wife Cathy, Stephen and I. The visitors consisted of his pastor, a nurse and a retired builder and his wife. Although it was a very pleasant time, it was a long way to talk to six people!

After breakfast, I chatted to the builder, who told me of his keen interest in mission work, and explained that he often went overseas on short-term assignments to do practical work for missionaries and their agencies. He also told me that his nephew worked for Samaritan's Purse; they provided support for medical projects around the world. I did not think either of these comments warranted much, but it was clear that Stephen's story had captured his attention and he was keen to help in whatever way he could. Then he left!

Later that morning, we had a call from our retired builder friend and he told us that he had called his nephew and had told him of the hospital. He had offered to help, but was involved in a major project called the 'Shoebox' – over

200,000 shoe boxes had to be packed into a container which was leaving at noon on the Monday for Africa. He would be working non-stop all weekend to meet this deadline, but if we sent an email to him and gave a brief outline of what we needed, he might be able to help.

Late on Saturday afternoon, we got a call from Samaritan's Purse to say they had read the email and wondered whether Stephen would like to visit their medical warehouse in Boon, South Carolina, on the Monday afternoon or Tuesday. We were scheduled to visit Elmbrook Church, Milwaukee on the Sunday and to be guests of Stuart and Jill Briscoe. Although I was flying back to the UK on the Monday, Stephen was not due to be in Dallas until Tuesday night to meet up with an Indian friend who happened to be a travel agent. A few telephone calls later, everything was arranged. Our travel agent friend arranged for Stephen to fly from Milwaukee to Boon on the Monday morning to visit Samaritan's Purse.

I knew nothing about Samaritan's Purse, except that Franklin Graham (Billy Graham's son) ran it. I hoped this would not be another wasted journey! In fact, the twenty-four hours in Boon was an important watershed in the life of the hospital, as it resulted in the hospital eventually being adopted as an official ministry project of Samaritan's Purse. In the years that followed, Samaritan's Purse funded the equipping and setting up of an eight bed Intensive Care Unit, a Neo-natal unit, a Diathermy unit and other invaluable equipment and resources. The value of their help is difficult to calculate but well in excess of one million dollars.

I often remember my feelings about the breakfast and how it was a waste of time, and what could a retired builder do to help us? I learnt an important lesson that morning. Never despise the small things, because little acorns grow into oak trees.

Adoniram Judson

by Philip Yancey

In preparation for the trip (to Burma), I read several biographies of Adoniram Judson, one of the first missionaries from the United States and the one who first brought the Christian faith to Burma. Hardship stalked his life. When war broke out with England, the Burmese arrested Judson because, light-skinned and English-speaking, he looked and talked like the enemy. (Actually, the U.S. was still recovering from its own war against England.)

Judson was force-marched barefoot for eight miles to a prison, where each night the guards passed a bamboo pole between his heavily shackled legs and hoisted the lower part of his body high off the ground. Blood rushed to his head, preventing sleep and causing fierce cramps in his shoulders and back. Clouds of mosquitoes feasted on the raw flesh of his feet and legs. Treatment like this went on for almost two years, and Judson managed to endure only because his devoted wife brought him food each day and pled with the guards for better treatment.

A few months after his release, Judson's wife, weakened by smallpox, died of a fever, and shortly after that their baby daughter also died. Judson nearly had a breakdown. He would kneel by his wife's grave for hours each day, regardless of weather. He built a one-room hut in the jungle, morosely dug his own grave in case it might prove necessary, and worked in solitude on a translation of the Bible in the Burmese language. Only a handful of Burmese had showed any interest in the Christian message. Yet he stayed on, thirty-four years in all, and because of his faithfulness more than one million Burmese Christians today trace their spiritual roots to Adoniram Judson. The dictionary he compiled, now nearly two hundred years old, remains the official dictionary of Myanmar.

But Who Gets the Credit? Us or Our God?

by Peter Meadows

In the sophisticated West it's hard to imagine a world that believes life is still subject to magic. Sure, we do live in a society rife with superstition and where more than a few have been bamboozled into thinking that David BlaIne and the like have something more going for them than 100 per cent trickery. But that's not what I mean.

Instead, picture a community where, almost to a person, they believe the answer to life is to find the most powerful God and keep him on your side. A community where simple scientific acts like finding water or growing healthy crops have 'Gods' – with 'personality' and 'feelings' at their heart.

And such a world most definitely exists. It's a world Christian development agencies encounter every day. And how they handle it makes a crucial difference to the way those they serve understand *why* they do what they do – and who they do it for.

Picture about thirty villagers standing under a baobab tree in northern Senegal. They're watching a World Vision soil scientist and a hydrologist working on the best site for a new borehole. The scientist is taking soil samples and his colleague is studying a hydrological survey spread over the bonnet of their car.

Of course, you understand perfectly what's going on. But what about those villagers? Chasing an answer you turn to your imaginary translator, *'What do you folks think these people are doing?'*

Comes the reply, *'That's simple. They are witch doctors. The one in the dirt is asking the spirit of the earth where the spirit of the water is. And the other one's consulting sacred texts, written in a secret language, just like our mullahs do.'*

'Are they any good?' you ask in shock. *'Oh, yes. They are better than our witch doctors. They always find the water'*. And they will.

You, the soil scientist and hydrologist are clear. The water was found by western science. But the locals explain the miracle of finding water though the lens of their traditional worldview. To them it must be magic, because there is no other rational explanation.

It was a chillingly bad moment when a Christian development agency found a village in India had added a further deity to their list of gods – complete with a shrine. It was chillingly bad because this new deity was them.

So what should the Christian agency say to the villagers in situations like this? If it is not magic, what is it? Say 'only science' and we contribute to the secularisation of their worldview. We move them towards a belief that only the physical and rational are real. But say nothing and we further reinforce their traditional worldview, leaving them to continue in their superstition. Neither is a Christian thing to do.

So what explanation can be truly Christian? The 'imaginary' situation above was actually the genuine experience of Bryant Myers, a World Vision Vice President. And it was he who first raised this issue in my mind.

I like Bryant's answer, though it may not always be easy to express or to have it believed. It's that the true God created a rational material universe. He also created us – those who come in Jesus' name to work alongside the poor – in his image. And therefore made us able to figure out how his world works and the natural rules it follows.

Such an explanation allows God to be God and also validates science as his creation. Fail to understand the need to explain things that way and we may not be being as Christian as we think we are. Or as Christian as we need to be.

Good News: Bad News

by Simon Vibert

You may have heard the story about the airline pilot speaking over the intercom to his passengers. The plane was going through some very stormy weather. The crew had already given indications that something was not quite right, they were racing up and down the aisles, and one passenger had looked out on the left of the plane and seen some smoke coming from one of the wings. Eventually, in order to allay the passengers' fears, the pilot announced, 'I apologise for all the commotion in the cabin, but I can say: I do have bad news for you but I have good news as well. The bad news is that the left engine is on fire, some very strong crosswinds have blown us off course, we are completely lost and it looks like we might need to land in the sea. But the good news is – we are making very good time!'

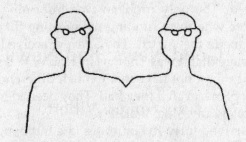

Pakistani Doppelganger

by Viv Thomas

In 1984 I was in the Punjab, working with a friend called Mike Wakeley. To many Pakistanis, Mike and I look much the same. We are both tall, English, wear glasses and are bald. Mike disguises his baldness better than I do but 'bald' describes us well. In reality, Mike and I are very different, both in background and personality but at an initial glance, in the middle of the Punjab on a dark night, in a sandstorm, we could be mistaken for each other.

Mike and I were working together on a number of projects and that meant speaking in churches and various Christian organisations around Pakistan. One afternoon, Mike asked me if I could speak that night in his place at a meeting two hours drive outside Lahore. I agreed. The only problem was informing the people who were running the meeting that we had made the switch. They never received the message that it was Thomas instead of Wakeley but it might not have made much difference to their plans, even if they had. They needed Mike Wakeley, any Mike Wakeley.

I arrived forty-five minutes late but bang on time if you live in Pakistan. To my surprise, there were over five hundred people gathered in this tent. I stood at the back while someone made an announcement in Punjabi. Then I heard the words booming out the microphone, 'Welcome Mike Wakeley'! Someone garlanded me and walked me down to the platform accompanied by thunderous applause. I sat at the end of a row of seven chairs, the seventh being mine. I whispered to the man next to me, 'I am not Mike Wakeley, I am Viv Thomas' but it was clear that he did not want to know. So I whispered again, 'I am not Mike Wakeley, I am Viv Thomas.' This time – after rolling his eyes into the top of his head – he took some action. While a man was singing a solo to the gathered crowd there was a rapid and earnest gathering of my six platform companions. My information had clearly caused a problem. While the solo continued, there was hand chopping and neck twitching as they sort to clear up the problem before the singer had finished. Everyone was captivated by the meeting on the platform and little attention was given to the poor singer.

Just as the solo finished, the six men sat down and I waited for my newfound eye-rolling friend to tell me what was the result of their deliberations. I was a little stunned by his next sentence. He leaned over and whispered, 'Do you mind if we call you Mike Wakeley?' I waited a second trying to sort out what was going on. Having to respond to his direct question, it was a time for a quick choice. So I said hesitatingly, 'No . . . I don't mind . . . call me Mike Wakeley if you want.' The anxiety dissolved from his face and was replaced by a smile as broad as the Sind Desert.

I suddenly realised the opportunity opening up in front of me. For tonight I could say whatever I wanted and Mike Wakeley would get the blame. I was free because of my doppelganger! Within twenty minutes it became clear that they needed Mike Wakeley – any Mike Wakeley – for they had a certificate of honour to present. Mike had raised some money for local redevelopment and this was their way of saying thank you. I stood at the appropriate time, was presented with my – sorry – Mike's certificate, and gave a humble speech of acceptance in the Mike Wakeley way. I had saved the face of my platform companions and everyone seemed happy. After my speech and on the way home I became Viv Thomas again but for a couple of hours it was a confusing joy being Mike Wakeley. Not for the first time in Christian history or revealed Scripture, something good had taken place through creative deception. Our attempts at holiness? I bet God laughs.

Homecoming

by Jeff Lucas

Tyler was sixteen when he died. He had lived in the valley of the shadow of death since he was eight years old, although it was not until his final year on earth that he learned just how terribly ill he was. The battle for Tyler began when, at the tender age of four, he developed neurofibromatosis – a disease that turns the body into a harrowingly efficient production line for tumours. Many suffer from this disability and live to tell the tale, but Tyler was one of the one per cent for whom this is not so. In fact, his was the worst case that the doctors could recall. His body was a mass of small predators, which conspired together to steal his ability to walk, birthing a brain tumour and robbing him of his right eye when he was just eight. He would endure twelve major surgeries and, in one six-week period, was unconscious beneath the scalpel for an unthinkable forty-nine hours. In the end, the doctors stopped counting tumours and counted days left instead. They knew that it would not be long.

For fourteen years, life said a firm 'no' to Tyler. His desire to play his beloved baseball was rudely declined: instead, he rode an electric wheelchair. He worked for a while in a skateboard shop, and would have been delighted to ride the sleek board they presented to him, but any hope that he might have had of whiling away balmy days surfing around the sidewalks with friends was cruelly dashed. Like any teenager, he dearly wanted to drive a car. But life's verdict has been firm, and without possibility of appeal: no. And his bike, which he had once been able to pedal furiously, was denied him too.

Unusually for one so young, Tyler's greatest ambition had been to become a father. Testament surely to the love of Josh and Sherri, his parents, Tyler longed to see his own children's laughing faces one day. When he was told that his disease was terminal, his first response surprised: 'I hope that I get to have kids first.' They said that, if he did live to become a dad, that his own offspring would have a fifty/fifty chance of being struck down by this terror disease. He determined that he would perhaps grow up to have one child, and adopt some more. But the prognosis was devastating, its cold accuracy correct – his hope of having children would never be. No.

And perhaps one of the toughest denials for the tactile Tyler was the fact that his family couldn't hug him anymore, a refusal born of kindness, not coldness, because to embrace him would have sent his nerves into searing agony. And he would watch longingly as Dad wrestled with his brothers and sisters; that rough-and-tumble playfulness way out of bounds for his fragile frame.

Despite all of the denials, Tyler was defiantly a 'Yes' person. His parents are quick to insist that he was no saint and, like us all, he had his moments where, like the rest of the human race, he could miss the mark. But for his disability, Sherri insists, he might have strolled into more trouble than he could navigate in a wheelchair. But there was gold produced in his furnace of pain as well. He determinedly pursued relationships, even when his telephone went quiet, as his school friends, not knowing what to say, how to act, stopped calling. He had a particular hankering to help a workmate who had a reputation for being a rough, tough guy, who had subsequently moved away. The night before he died, Tyler received a call from that long-distance friend, who insisted on coming to see him, and they spent an hour together that final evening.

Tyler said 'Yes' to what others saw as 'No' situations. When he was forced to abandon his regular bike, his dad took him and bought him a three-wheeled version in bright yellow. Depressed that his son would be reduced to an uncool three wheeler, Josh felt gloomy about the yellow machine, until Tyler blurted out on the way home: 'I am so blessed! I have got a three-wheeled bike!' No irony or sarcasm here, just gratitude, and celebration in the face of indignity. If his sight became dim, his humour stayed razor sharp. One night, as he sat with his family in the kitchen, all faces stained with tears, he announced that the 'Sob Fest', as he dubbed it, should come to an end. 'How about we all jack it in and go to bed?' he suggested. He gave Josh a ring with the single word 'Dad', printed on it, prompting yet more sobbing. Later, he held out his own hand, pretending that there was a ring there and mimicked his father's crying with a grin.

They asked him if he would like to go on a dream trip and, as many chronically ill children have done, he chose to go to Disney World. But there's a detail to note here: it was impossible for Tyler to go on a single ride; again, to do so would have bought waves of pain. His family knew that he had put in the request for their sake.

Sherri wanted to explain to her son that there was a bright future, out of this world, ahead. She compiled a book about his life, calling it 'Buckets of Glory'. The rationale was simple; she figured that her boy had been drenched with hundreds of buckets of suffering and pain. The Bible teaches that the glory out there will far outweigh and outshine any suffering down here. The maths is simple – there would be hundreds and hundreds of glory buckets waiting for her Tyler.

There was one other hope that Tyler had cherished. He had liked a girl in his church for a very long time. Erica is blonde and beautiful, with a warm, winning smile and a tender heart for God. In America, the football season begins with a so-called 'homecoming' party. Tyler asked Erica if she would do him the courtesy of accompanying him to this very special event. Somehow, the news of the proposed date got around the town. Two limousine companies called to offer the finest transport available, free of charge. A local florist provided the most beautiful bouquet to crown the evening. A jeweller gave an earring and necklace set for Tyler to present to his date – and three restaurants called to offer free dinner. But the big question remained: would Erica say 'Yes' to the date?

Tyler returned home from the hospital, to discover that his front garden had been totally transformed. Erica's family had pitched in to create a garden-wide carnival of colour. Bright balloons bounced in the breeze. Bunting garlanded the hedges. But what demanded Tyler's attention, as he stared, speechless, at the garden, was the dozens of fluorescent posters that had been placed everywhere. Many of them carried just one word, bold and arresting.

YES. YES. YES. YES.

Tyler, resplendent in his rented tuxedo and top hat, and the lovely Erica were transported to the party like royalty. He danced with her by flipping the joystick of his electric wheelchair backwards and forwards. It was a wonderful evening, when, just for once, life said a big 'Yes'.

And now, as you read this, Tyler is gone, his battle with the tumour machine that had been his body finally over. Sherri and Josh sensed that, as parents, they were about to witness what they saw as a real privilege – the entrance of their son into heaven. Three gifts were given to Tyler as he ended his life here. He had been completely deaf for five months, but, towards the end, he was able to hear the faintest whisper, the quiet reassurances of Mum and Dad as they prepared him for the great journey. And then, the night before he went, he reported hearing a voice, calling his name: a summons from above to the party? Finally, he was granted the gift of giving, even as he died. He was urgently insistent that his parents should not be alone when he died, and waited for help and support to come before he slipped peacefully away. And, as his family, including siblings Jeremy, Charlie, Katie and Colby gathered together, six of them to whisper their farewells for now, he deliberately went around the circle of them, pointing specifically at each one and, in sign language, using hands that he could barely move because of pain just the day before, he spelled out, 'I love you'. They whispered, 'We release you'. And as he flew away, they said that the sense of peace in the room was thick, tangible.

Something tells me that, when he skipped up the pathway to be with Jesus, the clumsy wheelchair an unnecessary accessory now, that the Lord himself wasn't the first sight he saw. Call me sentimental if you like. But, knowing Jesus, I reckon that Tyler had a special 'homecoming' party in heaven: a few billion bright buckets, brimming over with glory; a bike with two wheels, not three. And perhaps, to welcome him, there was a rash of a million bright posters on display, each one with just one word scrawled upon it.

'Yes'.

Tyler is home.

The Marks of Salvation: India

by Stephen Rand

At 8 p.m. the water level at the nearby Khodiar dam was rising alarmingly. When the power failed throughout the region the authorities at the dam panicked and opened the sluice gates. Within seconds an eight foot wall of water had crashed down on Vankiya. Large parts of the village were simply washed away. Scores of people had drowned.

Early the next morning we returned to the village to take pictures so we could illustrate the tragedy. I was taken to meet Gobar Madha. The rest of the villagers thought we would want to hear his story. He was sitting on a wall, unmoving, his eyes empty and staring. A little boy sat on his knee. Gabaru was five years old. When Gobar Madha heard the roar of the approaching water somehow he had grabbed Gabaru and started to climb a tree. The water had surged round him and he had felt the current tugging at his son's body.

In his desperation he was using both his hands to cling to the tree. He had sunk his teeth into the boy's shoulder, and for two hours they had held on together until the wind and the water began to drop. When it was safe to come down from the tree, Gobar Madha had discovered that his wife, brother, sister-in-law and eleven children had all been swept away and drowned. All that remained of his extended family was himself and Gabaru. Gobar Madha still sat, seemingly almost in shock. One of the villagers opened Gabaru's shirt so we could see the scars in his shoulder, a kind of fatherly stigmata, the marks of salvation.

Breakfast in Singapore

by Keith Danby

Visiting Singapore is a most enjoyable experience. It is a nation of three million people compacted into five square miles. With most of the population housed in high-rise apartments blocks, the Singaporeans live well ordered and disciplined lives. The most fascinating experience of all, though, was at meal times. Singaporeans eat out even more than Americans.

One morning I was taken to a food hall for breakfast. The first thing that struck me was that the building was circular in shape, with all the tables situated in a inner centre circle which was packed with people. The second thing I noticed was the noise and buzz in the hall. Around the outside were numerous kitchen kiosks, each offering their own speciality. It was quite normal to order one dish from one kiosk and another dish from another. What particularly intrigued me was there was table service, and each kiosk would send their server to your table to take the order. Once the server had taken the order, instead of walking back to the kitchen with the order, the server would shout the order to a person at the kitchen, giving a table number. What appeared to be anarchy was actually a well-organised system. Moments later the order was brought to the table, freshly prepared and piping hot.

Puzzled by such a system, I asked my host, 'How can the kitchen hear the order over all the other noise of the building?' The answer seemed obvious to my friend, who simply said they knew the voices of their people.

This became an important life-long lesson to me and gave me an important insight to a scripture which had always concerned me. In the hustle and bustle of life with so much going on, how does God hear my cries for help and know what I am saying to him? Also, in the juggling of our lives, how do we hear his voice? Simple. He knows the voices of his people. 'My sheep hear my voice.'

An Ordinary Girl Made Good

by Rodney Hui

'We have here only five loaves of bread and two
fish' – Disciples
'Bring them here to me' – Jesus

(Mt. 14:17, 18 NIV)

We were sitting at the Starbucks Café enjoying
our lattes. Of medium height, she looked ordi-
nary for a Singaporean. Her complexion would
have been fair if not for the past few years living at high altitude. As we started talking, the
drive she exuded and the passion she expressed
soon dispelled any thought of her ordinariness.

Before joining OM, Jane (not her real name)
ran her own accounting firm. She majored in
Mathematics at university but realised earlier
on that her nature was more suited to be a
social worker.

'I am highly motivated and practical,' Jane
described herself. 'And I think I am both task
and relationship oriented.' This sounded con-
tradictory. How that was possible she had no
idea, but she just knew. Her sense of optimism

and cheerfulness was infectious. 'I am also a simple girl – in material and in philosophy.' Another contradiction? Colleagues and staff said she was serious with her work, but fun to work with at the same time. They knew it because they had seen her love for them.

So how did a mathematician turned accountant turned 'tent-maker' in Nepal ended up in missions in the first place?

Jane became a Christian when she was fourteen years of age. At eighteen, she sensed God's calling for her into missions at a church missions conference. A desire was sparked in her heart to work in the third world. But the question uppermost on her mind was, where?

The answer came in 1997 at a Direction (missions) Camp run by OM. There, she heard about OM's need of a bookkeeper in Nepal. Although she had preferred a ministry rather than an administrative role, she did not mind as the position was on a part-time basis. The rest of the time could be used for ministry.

Like most Singaporeans from a Chinese family, she faced parental objection initially. But after the initial shock, her parents left the decision to her.

Upon arrival in Nepal, she did become the bookkeeper in the first year and she did get involved in the evangelistic work, just as she was promised. It was a good compromise that had worked out quite well. After the first year, she became the leader of the team of seven ladies. Leading a team involved planning duties, activities and seeing to each member's welfare and development. Some of the team members taught English to Nepalis, others helped out at children's centres, but all were involved in friendship evangelism – this involved befriending people, developing meaningful friendships and finding opportunities to share the gospel with them.

In the course of her ministry, Jane was requested by a Nepali co-worker to look after Dilu. Dilu, like many Nepali women, was a single mother. Her husband was an alcoholic in the village and one time, in his drunken stupor, set his son on fire. Later he simply disappeared from the village. Like many Nepali women, Dilu was illiterate and unskilled. With a son to look after and without the resources to put him through school much less in a children's home, she was in desperate need. Jane's job was to provide the care, support and friendship that Dilu needed.

There was a sewing project run by another Christian outfit from which Dilu was able to learn some sewing skills. Having learned to sew, Dilu was still unemployed. To help her out, Jane forked out US$30 from her own pocket, bought some materials and some samples of handicrafts from the market and got Dilu to sew some replicas. When Dilu was done, Jane set out to sell some of the finished products – mainly Nepali coin pouches.

'Friends bought the finished products out of sympathy!' mused Jane. With the profit from the sale, she gave some to Dilu and the rest was used to purchase more materials to make more pouches. This private arrangement steadily grew and Dilu began to earn some income that she could live on.

Then an idea struck Jane.

'If I could do it for one lady,' thought Jane, 'why not for two?' So another woman was recruited. In the course of time, more were added to the number.

Having people buy the products didn't mean that the products were of a high quality, observed Jane. If the products were not of a high quality, the business would quickly fail. The goal was to improve on the quality – to bring them to a marketable and compatible standard with those that were already in the market. The challenge was to bring the business to a sustainable level in the long-term.

The handicraft business has since grown. After several years of experimenting and learning, the quality of the handicrafts is compatible and they are easily sold to NGOs, Christian organisations and some souvenir shops.

'Business prospered when we found a niche and a demand for the services or products,' said Jane, sounding like a business guru. The same principle may also be applied in the missions context – in that when the fundamental needs of people are met, ministry prospers.

Today, there are twenty women working at the craft centre. 'The centre symbolises hope,' she declared. 'I want to bring hope to these women.' This group of women came from terrible backgrounds. Some are single mothers who had been physically abused by their husbands while others had run away to escape ill-treatment, only to discover they had nowhere to turn. There are also widows among them. Some were ex-prostitutes. Many have children but were without resources to see them grow like normal kids. All are genuinely appreciative of the employment that the centre provides.

Thus began what has now become a small and self-sustained cottage industry.

'My strategy is simple,' Jane admitted, 'what we make must be sold; products must be moved. They are not allowed to accumulate.' This way, the business is solvent financially. From selling to sympathetic friends and local contacts, the market is being expanded. The cheaper prices and better quality mean they have been able to carve a niche in the market. The main worry is that products like these last a long time and people don't think of replacing them so quickly.

And all this started because of a misunderstanding.

'At that time,' Jane told the story, 'my Nepali was limited.' When Dilu shared a dream she had with her, she misunderstood it as God wanting Dilu to learn to sew. Later, when her Nepali was better, she finally understood that Dilu was trying to tell her that the dream she had was about God using her to start a sewing ministry! Even in a misunderstanding, God worked.

Later, Jane was faced with a dilemma with Dilu, who had shown no improvement in her sewing skills. She simply could not upgrade. In the end, Jane helped her set up a small restaurant. Unfortunately, she started selling cheroot and alcohol, the same items that had nearly destroyed her life earlier on. With Dilu, as with all the women under her charge, Jane learned woman-management skills!

Some time later, a short-term team visited Nepal. Joe, one of the team members, after learning what Jane was doing, suggested to her the idea of making and selling soap. Joe informed her that JoJo, his wife, was very knowledgeable and might be able to help.

'I shelved the idea as soon as I heard it,' Jane said. Busyness in the ministry and the constant attention given to the handicraft centre was occupying much of her time and energy. Also, her (expiring) visa situation was looming at the back of her mind. After four years, she was still on an annual, renewable student visa. This did not give stability and assurance of continuity. A way must be found to obtain a longer term business visa to enable her to remain.

On the next visit to the immigration office, her fears were confirmed. Foreigners were not given business visas for handicraft and carpet industries. These are uniquely Nepali in nature, she was told. As a last resort, Jane suggested to the immigration officer – how about handmade soap? To her surprise, the answer was affirmative. The manufacture of soap is relatively unknown in Nepal. The idea of the transfer of this technology to Nepal was welcomed. A five-year business visa, renewable every year, was issued to her. The next thing for her to do was to start the soap business! What began as an idea had to be followed up with some concrete plans.

'I started finding out how to make soap, fast!' Jane exclaimed. On a trip to Britain for a leadership course in the seaside retreat centre in Wales, she bought a book on how to make soap. She read and soaked up everything on this subject. She learned everything needed to be learned about soap-making. She wanted to be practical too. Her first attempt at making soap was great in presentation but failed miserably in quality. She also corresponded with Robert, a Singaporean businessman, who was helpful with his advice and input.

'When I returned to Kathmandu, I experimented in earnest,' giggled Jane. 'At first, I thought there were only two types of soap: solid bar and liquid. As I found out more, the information forever changed the way I buy soap.'

Seldom do we think about soap as a load of chemicals, but it is. She gave this information: 'Each day we apply a whole host of chemicals on to our skin. No wonder some people, adults as well as children are allergic to soap!' Chemicals are used in commercial soap to give it colour, lather, smell and hardness.

'I learned,' volunteered Jane, 'that most commercial soap is made with animal fat. I do not fancy applying lard on to my face!'

As a result of her study, research and experiment, she came up with a formula that is 100 per cent natural. Her soap is made from a mixture of vegetable and essential oils, which are extracts from flowers.

When asked how her soap is made, she refused to disclose her trade secret except for these general steps – first, you mix oils and alkaline at the right temperature. Then you enhance the soap with a combination of oil and essential addictives. Stir until the mixture thickens. Then, pour it into moulds. Next comes the insulation of the moulds. When the soap is hardened, hand cut it. It is then cured for as long as three weeks. Finally, the soap is trimmed by hand. And by hand each piece is individually wrapped. The labels are self-printed and handcut. 'Believe me,'

Jane concluded, 'refining the technique and process took time!'

It was a year of trial and error. Commercial and large-scale soap producers use machines but Jane only had simple womenfolk to do the job.

Like the handicraft centre, the soap venture provided employment for other women in need. All ingredients and materials used are natural. The uniqueness is that no preservatives are used. 'From the start to the finish,' she declared, 'everything is handmade.'

For this enterprise, Jane rented a three-storey building. The factory is on the first floor, the office on the second and her accommodation is on the third. From a small group of women workers, the little factory now employs twenty-seven women and five men. The men make purchases, including the import of ingredients from overseas. Sales are also improving, with a steady and increasing demand coming from Singapore and other countries. The contacts are made each time she visits home.

What is it like running two businesses? Her reply underlined the ethos: 'We are like a big family. We talk about family matters, sing and talk some more in the course of our work.' The women are especially touched when Jane provides the personal care for them.

What are some of the struggles that come with such work?

'People are still people,' sighed Jane. 'They backbite, they are unhappy even when I help.' It was disheartening at times. There was a deaf and dumb girl who accused her of not feeding her and of withholding her money. Another struggle is the difficulty in recruiting long-termers to work with her. Short-term volunteers provide only short-term assistance and relief. The culture is also a challenge.

'The Nepali culture is so laid-back. I am type A – the activist. None of my workers is type A!'

When a ministry is going well, the enemy counter-attacks. Several articles in the local papers were written accusing her of proselytising. A rival, who had poached some of her workers, had also stolen her trade secret. This same person had orchestrated events that led to the reversal of her visa. A Nepali lawyer was engaged to deal with this situation while she waited for the outcome outside of Nepal. Not long after our meeting in Starbucks, the good news came that she had won the court case. She is preparing her return.

But what keeps her going?

Jane finds great satisfaction when she sees the quality of life improving among the women. It is a great encouragement for her to see single mothers now with the ability to buy food with their own money and send their children to schools. It is also good to see mothers and children putting on weight. This means they are getting the nutrition that they lacked before. Jane sees that God loves them practically.

But the greatest thrill is to see some coming to know the Lord. There is a lady who came to the Lord while working with her. She started sewing at the handicraft centre, but it soon became obvious that she couldn't sew. Another job was found for her – working as a maid. According to Jane, this lady has kept in contact and started bringing friends, and then her own sister, to the Lord. The chain effect is heartwarming.

In the future, Jane would like to see Nepali taking over the handicraft centre and the soap business. Her goal is to see both centres self-sufficient.

Her motivation is still to help more people find employment so that they may find dignity in their self-sufficiency and, in so doing, find the Lord.

The Neighbour

by Philip Yancey

I have a neighbour who is obsessively neat. He lives on ten forested acres, and every time he drove up his long, winding driveway, the disorderly dead branches on the Ponderosa pine trees bothered him. One day he called a tree-trimming service and learned it would cost him five thousand dollars to trim all those trees. Appalled at the price, he rented a chain saw and spent several weekends perched precariously on a ladder cutting back all the branches he could reach. He called the service for a new estimate and got an unwelcome surprise, 'Mr Rodrigues, it will probably cost you twice as much. You see, we were planning to use those lower branches to reach the higher ones. Now we have to bring in an expensive truck and work from a bucket.'

In some ways, modern society reminds me of that story. We have sawed off the lower branches on which western civilization was built, and the higher branches now seem dangerously out of reach. 'We have drained the light from the boughs in the sacred grove and snuffed it in the high places and along the banks of sacred streams,' writes Annie Dillard.

Flight BA52, Mumbai Airport: September 1996

by Keith Danby

It was one of those experiences everyone fears; arriving at your destination without your bags. I had checked in two bags at Heathrow, one with my clothes and the other with some seminar notes for a conference I was speaking at in Hyderabad in a few days' time. I had waited anxiously until the last bags came through the carousel. Still no sign of any of them! Then I recognised the very last bag. It was an old PVC soft-sided case, which had seen better days. I had put the two hundred seminar notes in this and did not intend to bring it home again. To my horror, the case had split apart and the notes were spilling onto the ground. I quickly retrieved the case and the contents and some-how managed to place it on the baggage trolley. Alas, no sign of the suitcase which had my clothes!

I was politely directed to the Customer Services desk for what turned out to be a marathon of form filling. I filled out forms to describe my suitcase, and its contents; the ticket details, the baggage tag details, where I embarked, where I disembarked, my address in England, my address in India, what I had for breakfast and what was my favourite colour! Just when I thought this was all about to be concluded, I was asked to go to the customs desk, as they were very interested in the contents of the bag that *had* arrived.

By this time, the airport was deserted. In Mumbai airport, only passengers are allowed in the terminal building, and I was becoming anxious that my friends who had come to meet me would be starting to think that either I had not arrived or that they had somehow missed me. I approached the counter in a hurry and with an air of importance. The Hindu lady on duty was about to give me a lesson in patience. She was on duty all night; did not have much else to do and clearly saw no reason to rush. Everything moved at a very slow pace. After about fifteen minutes, which felt like hours, I realised that the lady actually wanted an incentive to process the papers a little faster. Now the dilemma! It was our policy not to give bribes. This required some creative thinking!

I knelt down to the case and pulled out a copy of my seminar notes. I then opened my passport to my picture page, stuck out my shoulders, lifted myself to my full height of 5 foot 9 inches, pulled out my pen and pointed to my picture and my name. Then I pointed to my name on the seminar notes and proudly touched my chest to emphasis that I was the author of these notes. I then signed the notes with my most impressive signature and handed the dear lady her personal copy. To my surprise, she turned and went into the back office. Now I was worried. What had I done! I could see through the doorway that the customs officer was having a conversation with what appeared to be her supervisor. Again, the conversation seemed to take forever.

Several minutes later, she returned and with a stern look on her face said 'Two!' I quickly took out a second booklet and signed it, gave it to her and I was out of there in a flash! The seminar notes were entitled, *How to Run a Christian Bookshop*, by Keith Danby.

Grace Abusers

by Jeff Lucas

I stood in the airport check-in line, dark clouds gathering in my heart as I waited. And waited. The prospect of yet another transatlantic flight spent with my legs wrapped around my neck for nine hours filled me with dread. I just wanted to be home. Airports are such lonely places, emotional black holes that are crammed full of people who have no desire to be there at all; they just desperately want to get home/on holiday/to the business meeting. And the notion that air travel is glamorous couldn't be more flawed: sitting strapped inside a silver tube with three hundred travellers, most of whom are fighting a losing battle against high altitude flatulence is hardly enchanting. I stepped forward to the ticket counter and wished that 'beam me up Scotty' was a usable prayer that could just get me home, *right now*.

In a second, the sun came bursting out behind the dark clouds, as the check-in agent spoke.

'Good morning Mr Lucas. I have good news – you've been upgraded to business class today.'

I wanted to kiss her. Indeed, I wanted to kiss everyone in the airport, dance a waltz, sing an excerpt from *The Sound of Music*, and laugh out loud over the airport PA system. Business Class! A big, comfy seat, all to myself, with champagne and edible food that looks and even tastes like food, and flight attendants who smile and don't walk up and down the aisle with a cattle prod and . . .

. . . This was going to be beautiful. Like a stunned lottery winner, I offered my grateful thanks and headed for the airport lounge, my heart dancing with heady exhilaration. Suddenly, the airport was a truly beautiful place to be, filled with lovely, friendly people – or so it seemed. The receptionist in the lounge smiled and asked me why I was so happy. Breathlessly, I told her my news – I had been upgraded!

I chatted with the receptionist for around fifteen minutes and she told me some strange news – that many passengers react weirdly when they get a free upgrade. One would think that everyone would be brimming with gratitude – upgrading is like the airline is giving you a cheque for a couple of thousand pounds, such is the difference between the ticket cost of flying coach and business. And yet, strangely, many people become haughty and aggressive when they discover that they are sitting in a better seat. They become loud, demanding and obnoxious – and some even threaten to report the person who has upgraded them! They abuse the grace that has been showered upon them and attack the very people who have shown them kindness.

I wondered if I have been a grace abuser. I have been freely, outrageously forgiven – but how willing am I to pass that grace around to those who irritate and offend me? Through the cross, God has granted me the ultimate upgrade – from a lost forever to an eternity loaded with the genuine luxury of closeness to Jesus.

I have encountered too many churches that have been ripped apart by people who know well how to sing *Amazing Grace*, but they themselves are graceless, emotionally shrivelled and mean. Experts in conflict resolution say that Christians can be the worst at dealing with disagreement. Perhaps that's because of our insistence that we drag God into every conflict and discord, demanding that he agree with *our* preference and opinion. Slogans and clichés abound when we fall out – we're not just irritated with each other, we're 'grieved in our spirit'. It's not just that the music on Sunday wasn't to our taste – suddenly, God himself must have put his hands over his ears: after all, we didn't like it – so surely *he* didn't.

Throw in a bucketful of emotive prophecies and a liberal sprinkling of spiritual superiority and you've got a recipe for total disaster.

The Bible is patently clear about our need not just to enjoy and receive grace, but to pass it around. The forgiven are commanded to forgive; we who must drive heaven to distraction with our idiotic, bumbling sinfulness are exhorted to put up with each other's foibles. We are objects of love, children of a God who is willing to trust us with everything, including the redemption of a planet. That should lead us to run from cynicism and genuinely to believe the best of each other. We will of course be disappointed. Far better that though, than to live a jaundiced existence, empty of hope or optimism.

Meanwhile, back in the airport lounge, another surprise was in store. Just five minutes before the flight, the friendly receptionist hurried up to me. With a huge smile, she whispered: 'I know you've already been bumped up to Business Class, but we need to move another passenger up – so I'm *double* upgrading you and putting you in First Class today. That means you get to sleep in a real bed and you get the best food available.'

My jaw almost hit the floor. Grace upon grace! The first-class seat would cost ten times the price of my ticket. I asked her why she had done it.

'It's simple. You were nice to me. Have a great flight.'

The Indicator of Prayer

by John Ortberg

It is striking to me how – both in scripture and in present-day examples – stories of water-walking are almost always stories about prayer. There is something about getting out of the boat that turns people into intense pray-ers, because they are aware that they cannot accomplish things without God's help.

One of my favourite adventures in prayer involves Doug Coe, who has a ministry in Washington, D.C., that mostly involves people in politics and statecraft. Doug became acquainted with Bob, an insurance salesman, who was completely unconnected with any government circles. Bob became a Christian and began to meet with Doug to learn about his new faith.

One day, Bob came in all excited about a statement in the Bible where Jesus says, 'Ask whatever you will in my name, and you shall receive it.'

'It that really true?' Bob demanded.

Doug explained, 'Well, it's not a blank check. You have to take it in context of the teachings of the whole scripture on prayer. But yes – it really is true. Jesus really does answer prayer.'

'Great!' Bob said. 'Then I gotta start praying for something. I think I'll pray for Africa.'

'That's kind of a broad target. Why don't you narrow it down to one country?' Doug advised.

'All right. I'll pray for Kenya.'

'Do you know anyone in Kenya?' Doug asked.

'No'.

'Ever been to Kenya?'

'No.' Bob just wanted to pray for Kenya.

So Doug made an unusual arrangement. He challenged Bob to pray every day for six months for Kenya. If Bob would do that and nothing extraordinary happened, Doug would pay him five hundred dollars. But if something remarkable did happen, Bob would pay Doug five hundred dollars. And if Bob did not pray every day, the whole deal was off. It was a pretty unusual prayer programme, but then Doug is a creative guy.

Bob began to pray, and for a long while nothing happened. Then one night he was at a dinner in Washington. The people around the table explained what they did for a living. One woman said she helped run an orphanage in Kenya – the largest of its kind.

Bob saw five hundred dollars suddenly sprout wings and begin to fly away. But he could not keep quiet. Bob roared to life. He had not said much up to this point, and now he pounded her relentlessly with question after question.

'You're obviously very interested in my country,' the woman said to Bob, overwhelmed by his sudden barrage of questions. 'You've been to Kenya before?'

'No.'

'You know someone in Kenya?'

'No.'

'Then how do you happen to be so curious?'

'Well, someone is kind of paying me five hundred dollars to pray . . .'

She asked Bob if he would like to come visit Kenya and tour the orphanage. Bob was so eager to go, he would have left that very night if he could.

When Bob arrived in Kenya, he was appalled by the poverty and the lack of basic health care. Upon returning to Washington, he couldn't get this place out of his mind. He began to write to large pharmaceutical companies, describing to them the vast need he had seen. He reminded them that every year they would throw away large amounts of medical supplies that went unsold. 'Why not send them to this place in Kenya?' he asked.

And some of them did. This orphanage received more than a million dollars' worth of medical supplies.

The woman called Bob up and said, 'Bob, this is amazing! We've had the most phenomenal gifts because of the letters you wrote. We would like to fly you back over and have a big party. Will you come?'

So Bob flew back to Kenya. While he was there, the president of Kenya came to the celebration, because it was the largest orphanage in the country, and offered to take Bob on a tour of Nairobi, the capital city. In the course of the tour they saw a prison. Bob asked about a group of prisoners there.

'They're political prisoners,' he was told.

'That's a bad idea,' Bob said brightly. 'You should let them out.'

Bob finished the tour and flew back home. Sometime later, Bob received a phone call from the State Department of the United States government:

'Is this Bob?'

'Yes.'

'Were you recently in Kenya?'

'Yes.'

'Did you make any statements to the president about political prisoners?'

'Yes.'

'What did you say?'

'I told him he should let them out.'

The State Department official explained that the department had been working for years to get the release of those prisoners, to no avail. Normal diplomatic channels and political maneuvrings had led to a dead end. But now the prisoners had been released, and the State Department was told it had been largely because of . . . Bob. So the government was calling to say thanks.

Several months later, the president of Kenya made a phone call to Bob. He was going to rearrange his government and select a new cabinet. Would Bob be willing to fly over and pray for him for three days while he worked on this very important task?

So Bob – who was not politically connected at all – boarded a plane once more and flew back to Kenya, where he prayed and asked God to give wisdom for the leader of the nation as he selected his government. All this happened because one man got out of the boat.

Jonathan Agunda: Standing Tall

by Cherie Rayburn

At twenty-one years old, Leadership Development Programme (LDP) student Jonathan Agunda is a small person accomplishing big things with God's help.

Although Jonathan is only 5 feet, 5 inches tall, he is unable to stand fully upright inside his home in Nairobi's Mathare Valley. Not unlike the other homes in this impoverished squatter's community, the one Jonathan shares with his mother and older sister is a small one-room structure with mud walls, a dirt floor and a corrugated tin roof. There is no running water, electricity or bathroom.

Kenya's Mathare Valley is not a place that inspires great accomplishments. It is where Nairobi's poorest congregate and slowly waste away from disease, starvation and lack of hope. But even in this desperate place, God can be found.

A Spark of Hope

'Compassion really gave me and my family hope for a better life,' says Jonathan, who was enrolled in a local church-based project when he was ten years old. Specifically, it was project worker Isaac Okinyi who instilled in Jonathan the confidence and desire to become all he could be in Christ. 'Mr Okinyi recognised my potential and immediately became involved in my academic life by encouraging me to do my best.'

Jonathan's best, as it turned out, was impressive. He was first in his class throughout his elementary and secondary school years. An outgoing boy, he also excelled at soccer and as a Sunday school teacher at the Redeemed Gospel Church. It was obvious that he had natural leadership ability and the potential to succeed in Compassion's Leadership Development Program.

Currently a second-year LDP student, Jonathan is succeeding, majoring in finance at Nairobi University and, at the same time, honing his Christian leadership skills.

The Confidence to Look Ahead

Looking ahead is not something the residents of Mathare Valley like to do. For too many of them, bowed under the weight of poverty, the future holds only despair. But in one Mathare home, a young college student stands tall, looking forward to a better life, one in which he can help ease the burdens of others and share with them the light and life of Christ.

And the Greatest of These is Toilets

by Richard Wallis

And now these three remain: spiders, snakes and toilets. But the greatest of these is toilets.

You will never forget your first encounter when on mission in Africa. For some, it is the western style toilets proudly displaying the Royal Doulton logo but with a flush mechanism that died a generation ago. Worse, there is no toilet brush or bleach in sight. For others, it is the tentative first steps into the pit latrine. First, you caution the new recruit – do not spray DOOM (the mind-boggling name for an African insect killing spray) down the hole as an army of cockroaches will emerge. Then you go through the technique: put on flip-flops, squat (I have found stretching out arms to nearest walls helpful) followed by the aiming skills of a Lancaster Bomber pilot. Swill surrounding area with a bucket of water and brush everything down hole. For me, my first encounter with a pit latrine was to prove to be a love affair. Such a simple and uncomplicated form of satisfaction.

I want to tell you a story of ghosts in white canvas, flying white teeth in a banana plantation and the official opening of a pit latrine.

The story begins with the Signpost International team waking up on the shores of Lake Victoria. We had been asked to be ready by 7 a.m. and stood together in awe as dawn broke over the lake. We were ready. Many of the team had been up late preparing messages for the convention we would travel to in western Uganda. At 10 a.m., we were still ready and waiting and feeling extremely hot. Eventually, a battered coach came to collect us. We were on our way – or were we? First to a depot to collect our tents. I had seen cannons from the Battle of Balaclava in England (there is one near Huntingdon station) but had no idea what happened to the tents from the Crimean campaign. As we crammed piles of faded white cloth, twisted rope, wooden poles and cracked pegs into the pick-up that would follow the bus, I realised where they had ended up. Now we were really on our way. Choruses boomed out of the coach's windows as we headed west.

Team leadership is never without complications – today it was young Lesley, with a rapidly swelling thumb, which had been bitten by an insect. We would need to find a clinic when we reached Mbarara. We parked up in Mbarara's market square on arrival at 4 p.m.. Mary Anne, who was acting as team nurse,

Lesley and I went in search of the nearest clinic, leaving a wilting team in the bus. Found a clinic. Queues to see a doctor, then the diagnosis, an injection and queues to pay the bill. Suddenly, night had fallen. How was the rest of the team? Was the bus still in the market place? For sure, morale would now be low in the stuffy bus – and it was more than fourteen hours since I had roused the team before dawn. This was my moment. Drawing on the best of Shakespeare, Churchill and St Paul, I prepared an inspirational speech to deliver from the steps of the bus. 'Once more unto the breach dear friends, once more . . . we will never give up . . . we must finish the race.' I strode with purpose across the market place towards the bus – Top Gun style. There comes a time in every leader's life when he must deliver. This was my moment.

'Hi Richard, we have had a brilliant time here – just amazing' was my greeting from the first group of team members I bumped into. 'Oh, really?' I retorted. 'Yes, we have been sharing the gospel with folk in the marketplace and some have become Christians.' Double take. Who needed a morale booster?

The journey continued in the darkness. The convention was planned to start at 3 p.m. and we would not reach our destination until nearly 9 p.m. Our dirt track took us through one banana plantation after another. At last, we saw the light of a hurricane lamp – we had arrived. Exhausted, we got off the bus and the first team members to descend thought they were hallucinating – they were greeted by a colony of white teeth. It was pitch black (no electricity for miles) and teeth was all they could see. As our African hosts saw our confusion, their teeth parted into huge smiles.

The story should end here – they slept happily ever after. But this is Africa! Drums were beating in the valley below.

The priority was to erect the tents which the 'boy scouts' in the team attempted to do by the light of the bus's main beams. But the instructions had been lost between the Crimea and Uganda, everything was tangled up, like a pile of fishing nets, and poles did not fit holes. The 'boy scouts' started drifting all over the banana plantation as they struggled with the tent over their heads – ghosts in white canvas. Our African hosts must have been staggered. We were the first *mzungus* (white men) to stay in their village and they must have been amazed by our nocturnal customs. Realising that my leadership was now in danger of total disintegration (I had once felt exceptionally clever after putting up a small Wendy House) I asked about the drums in the valley. 'Ah Richard, this is the 3 p.m. session. They are waiting for you to preach.' Sometimes God is exceptionally good. I left the team playing ghosts with a slightly spiritual: 'I am off to share the word down in the valley.'

I was the first up the following morning – we had been woken by the four hundred convention delegates prayer-marching past our sagging tent at 5.30 a.m. My guess was that everyone else had followed my practice the previous night and found a banana tree for their night time constitutional. But now it was morning and I am a regular sort of guy. I asked a senior pastor what was available. 'Oh, Pastor Richard, we have been waiting for this moment. The villagers have built a new pit latrine for the team in the village square. Please come and open it now.' I grabbed my flip-flops and after the briefest of speeches, I entered the holy of holies. With arms stretched wide holding onto sacks inscribed USAID, I peered through the chinks in the sackcloth, observing the crowd awaiting for me to emerge.

I never did give my speech from the steps of the bus. But I did open a new pit latrine in Africa. I think God was amused by that exchange.

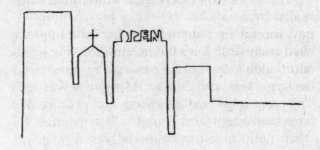

It's a Complex Issue,
the Edifice Complex

by Peter Meadows

When it comes to responding to poverty there are some seemingly simple no-brainers. And mostly they involve bunging up a building. An orphanage or two, a school or three. A hospital or six.

There's a need, so let's build something. But is this always the best we can do when addressing need? To send forth or fund a plethora of builders in Jesus name? All the while imagining we have done our best! There are big issues here, for those who cough up the money, those who put it to use and those on the receiving end.

For a start, how often is our thinking conditioned by what donors are the most willing to pay for rather than what poor communities need and want? Let's face it, buildings are solid and tangible things you can photograph, visit, declare open and produce detailed plans for. They are also things we understand because we have them ourselves.

In contrast, you can't photograph a range of newly acquired skills, strategies or abilities. Or stick a plaque with your name on a community's increased ability to care for the most needy among them, to better negotiate with their landlords or local civil authorities for improved conditions, or to resolve longstanding conflicts with their neighbours that are hindering their progress.

But a permanent, tangible, photographable and visitable edifice to our generosity is something different. It's something about which we can say 'we did that' – with pride.

Second, buildings are an easy, hardly-worth-a-second-thought solution. Education, healthcare, the care of orphans and those with special needs all need a roof over their head. Don't they?

As you struggle to say something other than 'of course' consider what painful experience in Cambodia over the past two decades has to say to us on the subject. When domestic unrest comes – and it's on the increase in our world

– what enduring value do walls and roofs offer when they collapse under bombs and tanks or when the people scatter for their lives?

Just suppose the same money, time and effort had been poured into giving the community knowledge, know-how, networks of skilled relationships and so on? Then there would have been something to sustain those in need wherever they were, buildings or not. Then they would have something no invaders could render worthless.

But what about orphanages? Are they the best idea? Or even a good one? In some communities, parents who are poor, though perfectly able to care for their young, willingly give away their children to be brought up under such a roof. For them it is the most loving thing to do. Which means there's an inexhaustible supply of children waiting for the orphanages we in the west just love to build and then have to go on funding year on year on year.

There's a better way, as agencies like World Vision have come to realise. It's to commit the same level of expenditure and expertise into helping the poor community enrich their lives to a level where they can care for their own.

In some settings even a school is not the best way to go. Take the community that said 'yes' to a school but left it almost empty of pupils when the opening ceremony was over, the bunting had been put away and the two hours of speeches had finally come to an end. Why? Because the local economy forced the children to be an essential part of the workforce. Without them sharing in working in the fields neither they nor their families would have had enough to eat.

Better than four walls and a roof would have been to spend the same money and effort on something un-photographable – like better seeds, alternative crops, training in more productive methods. All the while making informal education available out of working hours.

Of course, there are exceptions to the 'don't build it' approach. There has to be a place for schools, hospitals and special-care homes – at the right time and in the right place. But this is no reason to park our brains and failing to ask whether all the buildings we in the west, and in the church, fund and erect are genuine 'exceptions'. Or if too many are simply the result of shallow, short-term, heart-jerk thinking – with a dose of western imperialism and our own edifice complex thrown in?

Indeed, will the day ever come when a UK church says, 'We are planning our own building project and would like to match the money we raise by supporting something in a poor community. Something like increasing the leadership and decision-making skills of the community's leaders'. I dream about it.

Birds of a Feather

by Jim Seybert

There is a species of tiny little birds who gather in great numbers to swarm over the surface of the ocean just off the coast of California. From the beach they appear amoeba-like. A black wave of feathers zooming back and forth at break-neck speed, just inches above the water.

I often wonder how it is that every bird knows the precise moment to change direction. There are quite literally thousands of them and they never bump into each other. You can observe similar behavior in flocks of geese, schools of fish, stampeding cattle – could it be the hand of a creator God?

29th Birthday Treat, Sri Lanka: February 1980

by Stephen Rand

'Would you like to go to the beach for a swim?' they asked. This was a hitherto unique offer for someone brought up in Birmingham with a February birthday. The alacrity with which I accepted was far more to do with imagining the impact of the report back home than any great love of swimming in the sea. 'Did you have a good trip?' 'Oh, yes, I had a swim in the Indian Ocean on my birthday, you know.' 'Really . . .'

I then almost as quickly remembered the main drawback of beach swimming. 'What about getting changed?' I thought of my small towel, my large body, my white skin and a possibly crowded beach. I can't remember exactly how it happened, but once I had established that the beach was only a short distance away, it seemed quite sensible to get changed in their house and then walk down to the beach. Again, I thought of my small towel, my large body and my white skin and decided that it would be wise to don my dressing gown for this short trip.

It was a pleasant cotton dressing gown, a tasteful mix of subdued red and blue stripes. With my towel round my neck, a hat perched on my head, flip-flops on my feet, I was ready for my short stroll down to the beach. It was not long before I realised I had missed out on two vital pieces of information. The first was that the short walk was actually along a main market street, with busy, bustling stalls hemming in the road from either side. The second was that I had not extracted any definition of the word 'short'.

Within seconds I recognised that I was now the main sight of interest in the entire street. It wasn't that everyone stopped to gaze; it just felt like it. My face reddened to a shade far less tasteful than any in my dressing gown stripes. I frantically concentrated on the produce on the stalls in an attempt to not think how absurd I must look: that's why I know one stall was selling imported swiss roll. And I desperately hoped that the beach would be just round the corner.

Perhaps it was. Time has a habit of feeling a different length to reality. It seemed to take about half-an-hour to force my way through the market crowds, every step a reminder that I would have to return the same way. Eventually, the market ended. We crossed a railway line and walked under the line of palm trees that fringed the beach. I caught a glimpse of the rats running about the trees, and heard a voice explaining that they climbed the trees and occasionally gnawed through the stem of the coconut, so that it came crashing down on the unwary passer-by. I reflected that this aspect of the Indian Ocean beaches was not often highlighted in the exotic holiday brochures.

The silvery sands of the beaches were; and this beach, once past the market and the rats, fully matched the pictures. It swept off to the horizon in both directions, almost completely deserted, and fringing the sea whose colour seemed to redefine blue with a whole new intensity. I removed my dressing gown and dashed for the water, hoping that my speed would not allow anyone to take in my white whale-like appearance and confident for once that it would not feel like running into a cold shower. It didn't. It was warm, it was pleasant. I swam and relaxed. I swam and relaxed a little more. I stayed in the water for a long time. This was my February birthday treat. I even managed to forget for a few minutes that I still had to walk back, past the rats and the market. I decided rats were quite fun after all.

Christian Persecution in the Muslim World

by David Alton and Michele Lombard

Before the events of September 11, 2001, few people in the western world knew much about the existence of militant Islamic extremists engaged in a jihad or 'holy war' against Christians, Jews and the West, and even less were aware of the passion of their hostility. Since then, the reality of religiously motivated 'terrorism' has become increasingly familiar. Unfortunately, Christians and other religious minorities throughout the Middle East, and parts of Asia and Africa, have been persecuted by Islamic governments and fundamentalist groups for years.

Week Two: Indonesia

Blessed are those who have been persecuted for the sake of righteousness, for theirs is the kingdom of heaven. Blessed are you when men cast insults at you, and persecute you, and say all kinds of evil against you falsely, on account of Me. Rejoice, and be glad, for your reward in heaven is great, for so they persecuted the prophets who were before you (Mt 5:10-12).

Indonesia is home to more Muslims than any country in the world. It also home to one of the most violent and militant Islamic extremist groups in the world: the Laskar Jihad, or 'holy war,' whose fighters include native Indonesian and outsiders including Afghans and Pakistanis. Laskar Jihad has infiltrated the provinces of West Papua and Sulawesi, both of which have large Christian communities. For three years following January 1999, estimates of upwards of 80,000 Christians were forced to flee their homes in Maluku and thousands subjected to forced conversion rituals. In Central Sulawesi, numerous attacks have been carried out against Christians; nearly 20,000 have been forced to flee their villages.

blessed

On April 28, 2002, in the Moluccan village of Soya, a massacre led by about a dozen attackers armed with automatic rifles, grenades and knives claimed the lives of at least twelve, including a tiny baby. Some of the victims were stabbed, some shot, and others burnt to death. Witnesses report that the callous assailants went from house to house, opening fire on whoever was at home. In addition to these brutal murders, the attackers set fire to thirty Christian homes and a Protestant church.

In August 2002, a number of Laskar Jihad attacks occurred in Poso, Central Sulawesi, Indonesia. On August 5, eighty to one hundred assailants dressed in black, like ninjas, attacked the Christian village of Makato. Four women and one man were shot; two others were seriously injured, and seven reported missing. Many houses and a church were set on fire during the attack.

Three days later, an Italian tourist was killed and four other people were injured by Muslims who attacked a passenger bus. The following day, all Christian homes in the villages of Malei and Tongko were set on fire. Then on August 11, five Christians were killed when the bus in which they were riding was hijacked. Four bodies were thrown from it as it drove through the streets of Kayamanya. On the same day, at least seventeen homes in the village of Rononuncu were burned to the ground.

The following day, two more Christian villages in Poso were attacked by Laskar Jihad fighters dressed in black and firing automatic weapons. The villagers, powerless to fight off their attackers, were forced to flee, leaving their homes to be plundered and burnt to the ground. Hundreds of homes were destroyed, two churches burnt down, and at least five persons killed in the attacks, while at least two others were critically injured.

Similar attacks occurred throughout the remainder of August 2002 in Mayumba, Morowalyu, and Bunta Toini. Bombs exploded in Gebangrejo, Kayamanya and Jalan Morotai Kelurahan Gebang, resulting in further deaths and destruction of property.

Three people were injured the following month when a bomb exploded at a Christian school in East Palu. In a related incident, Reverend Rinaldy Damanik was arrested on false charges when he voluntarily reported to the Central Post of Indonesian National Police to provide testimony with regard to the Laskar Jihad attacks on these six villages in Poso. He was arrested on arrival as police claimed that he had always been a suspect and was thus to be detained.

Despite having failed to substantiate any charge against him, police extended his detention indefinitely because of pressure from political opportunists and religious extremists. This additional unlawful detention began on October 2, 2002, and has been marked by multiple and continued efforts to falsely establish his guilt. Despite these legal violations, Reverend Rinaldy Dimanak was sentenced to three years imprisonment on charges of illegal weapons possession on June 16, 2003. In August 2003 his appeal to the High Court was denied. Jubilee Campaign will continue to work for his unconditional release.

The Laskar Jihad intends to Islamicise all Indonesia by force, changing its pluralist constitution to an Islamic one, and imposing strict Islamic Shari'a law as the law of the land. This strategy is already being enforced in the Christian areas of the Moluccas and Sulawesi, and is likely be imposed on West Papua soon. Forced conversion to Islam or utter annihilation is the choice facing Indonesia's Christian minority. It appears that Indonesia's government and military are both unwilling and unable to do anything to stop the dangerous, brutal Laskar Jihad gaining in strength and power in its war on Christians.

Although thousands of native Indonesians have been murdered at the hands of the Laskar Jihad, the international media paid little attention until the October 12, 2002 bombing at a night club in Bali. That bombing, which bears a striking similarity to the tactics of the Laskar Jihad and its sister organization,

Al Qaeda, claimed nearly two hundred innocent lives.

Elliot Abrams, Chairman of the US
Commission on International Religious Freedom,
sent a letter to US Secretary of State Colin Powell
on February 16, 2003. In it, he stated: 'The
Indonesian Government has not controlled its
armed forces or the influx of armed groups from
other islands, reportedly resulting in murder,
forced mass resettlement, forced conversion to
Islam, and torture.' Abrams recommended that
the United States open debate on the issue.

Prayer Points:

• Please pray for the protection and deliver-
  ance of Christians in Indonesia; that they will
  be strengthened in their faith and comforted
  in their suffering; that God in his mercy will
  spare them from further unspeakable horror,
  and raise up intercessors and advocates to
  lighten their heavy burdens.
• Please pray for an end to the bombings, the
  attacks, the massacres, and the destruction of
  homes and churches by the Laskar Jihad,
  other Islamic groups and the Indonesian
  Military; for an end to unjust arrests and
  imprisonment, and the release of Reverend
  Rinaldy Damanik and other Christians who
  have been unjustly imprisoned.

- Please pray that Indonesia's leaders take a firm stand against the Islamic terrorists operating in their midst; that Shari'a law is not imposed, but that just laws and the rule of law are established and upheld in Indonesia; that the Indonesian Government, inspired by prayer and the encouragement and example of Christians throughout the world, will protect the lives and religious freedoms of its minority citizens.

Desire Less

by Philip Yancey

'There are two ways to get enough,' said G.K.
Chesterton; 'one is to continue to accumulate
more and more. The other is to desire less.'

Church in a Place of Famine: Burkina Faso

by Stephen Rand

We visited Guibaré on a Sunday, which gave us the opportunity to experience some African worship. The sermon was about prayer, illustrated from the story of Elijah when the drought is broken; there was fervent prayer for rain and equally fervent prayer for people to be saved. But the highlight of the service was the offering. A bowl was placed on the floor at the front of the church; a drum began to beat, and people shuffled and danced their way to the front to make their gift, many of them actually smiling. I was still trying to come to terms with this culture shock, when the full bowl was replaced by an empty one and the drum started up again. Once again people shuffle-danced up to the front, and once again notes and coins were placed in the bowl. 'What's the second offering for?' I asked our interpreter. The answer left me slightly stunned: 'The first was the tithe; the second is their thank-offering.'

A Lifelong Servant of God

by Yamamori and Chan

Some of God's servants have been called to
spread the gospel in China's remote regions.
Many new Christian communities have been
born out of their hunger, torture, illness, jail, lone-
liness, poverty and humiliation. They embody the
spiritual strength of the church in China –
endurance in suffering. Lu Bingzhi, now in her
nineties, was like thousands of Chinese evangel-
ists who overcame the fiery trials of the twentieth
century to lead many to Christ through their
words and lives. Below are some of the fragments
of events critical in Lu's spiritual journey, as told
to Rev Yang Meiyong of Kunming, Yunnan.

In 1909, Lu Bingzhi was born to Christian parents
in Shangdong province, eastern China. Despite
their prayers, Lu refused to accept Christianity.
Once when she heard her father praying for her
salvation, this high school girl angrily said, 'I will
not believe this Jesus, which you believe in.'

Very soon, however, an ulcer developed on
her left leg. It began to grow and her family

could not pay for medical treatment. Soon, the doctors recommended amputation to save her life. Her parents earnestly asked God to spare their daughter from becoming a handicapped person. Strongwilled but desperate, Lu also knelt with her parents to pray for God's mercy and to confess her sins. Her leg was completely healed, and Lu realised that she had to accept this Jesus. Lu knew that her previous anti-Christian words were spoken in ignorance, but she would not dare to offend her Creator again, and she committed her life, suddenly transformed, to this God of mercy. She became a messenger of the good news she had received.

At this time, China was racked by civil war between various warlords and between the Communists and the Nationalists. Eventually, Lu travelled to northwestern China. For a while, she conducted evangelistic ministries at seven university campuses, leading students to Christ. However, the Nationalists suspected her of being a Communist agent, organising underground cells among the students. Without any investigation, they arrested Lu and sentenced her to death.

The jailer told her, 'I sympathise for you, for you are so young. We have to execute you very soon. I can pass on a message to your parents if you wish.' Lu replied, 'I am innocent. I preach Jesus Christ, not politics. If my God is not willing (for me to die), not one single hair of mine will fall on the ground. I will not die.'

Fu Zuoyi, the northwestern regional commissioner general, heard of the death sentence given to a young lady and asked to see her. After he interviewed Lu, General Fu said, 'This is a preacher of Christian religion. We should not execute her and should immediately release her.' Lu's confident trust in her God had been well placed. The governor, apologetic, even hosted a dinner in her honour.

God protected Lu in various ways. Once, during winter, she was on her way to do evangelism. For some reason, the horse she was riding would not go on the road but only on a frozen river bed. Lu tried to pull the horse back to the road but it would not yield. Later, however, it returned to the road. Lu could not understand why. Just after that, some Christians at the roadside welcomed Lu, telling her that a group of bandits had been waiting by the way. In fact, some travellers had just been robbed. Lu was convinced that God had sidetracked the horse to spare her. When Lu was twenty-two, she rode alone on a white horse to Saerqin in Inner Mongolia to preach the gospel. 'Many people tried to convince me not to go there because there were many bandits there, and they would do all kinds of evil things,' she said. 'It would be very dangerous. But, after prayer, I started my journey.'

In the area were some notorious bandits from Shangdong, led by a man called Big Pox Liu. The government had tried to suppress them, without success. As Lu rode on, she came upon a group of men. 'They ordered me to dismount from the horse and saw that I was a girl,' she recalled. 'They said, 'What are you doing?' I replied, 'I am an evangelist preaching the gospel of Jesus Christ.' They said 'How can a young girl like you preach?' I boldly said 'Step aside and let me pass, otherwise the bandits will come.' They laughed and said 'We are the bandits! You just bumped into us today.' Then I pleaded, 'Let me go. If you do not believe me, come to Saerqin Town tomorrow and hear my preaching.' I also told them I was from Shangdong. They said that since this young girl was from Shangdong, they would come to hear what kind of teaching I would offer.'

The bandits let her go. The following day, they came to Lu's preaching station. Then the whole gang, led by Big Pox Liu, knelt down and cried, confessing all their sins. Next they asked Lu: 'What shall we do now?' She told them to surrender their weapons to the government, so they went to see Inner Mongolia's provincial governor. They told him that after hearing this Shangdong girl's message of Jesus, they wanted to surrender and start a new life. Surprised, the governor declared that the government would accept their surrender. He pardoned them and gave them a piece of land to farm.

The change in Liu and his people was real. They had a good harvest after the first year and offered it to the government as an expression of their sincerity. The governor, however, declined to accept the harvest, knowing that they would need it. He even exempted them from land tax for the first three years. Liu and his people worked hard to show their repentance. They also led 300 people to Christ. There was peace in that region and God's name was glorified.

In 1942, Lu attended the Jinan Bible School; later, she transferred to North China Theological Seminary. When time permitted, Lu and her classmates would do evangelistic work in the countryside. In 1946, she was a faculty member at the Nanjing Huangnegang Theological Seminary. She was also in charge of the devotional ministry in eleven schools in Nanjing. The work was busy and tiring, but her preaching was powerful and many came to Christ.

One day, while praying, she saw a map of China in a vision. Soon, everything on it faded except Kunming City in Yunnan. Lu knew that the Lord was leading her there and shared her vision with her co-workers. Some joined her. In 1948, Lu and her co-workers arrived at Kunming. Soon, they rented a place on the Wuguo Road and started preaching. Many people accepted the Lord, and soon Lu and company had to find a larger place. The believers kept increasing in number. In 1952, two years after the Communist Party came to power, Lu and her co-workers bought a long hall with thirteen houses so that more people would hear the gospel. Soon after, however, the meetings were banned, and Lu and many other pastors were arrested.

Imprisoned, Lu became ill. As her health improved, she was transferred to a prison farm. Despite heart and stomach problems, every day she had to collect a certain amount of tea leaves from the mountain. Work began at 6 a.m. and ended at 8 p.m. If she could not fulfil her quota, she would be punished. One winter evening, Lu finished rather late. Alone, she met five wolves on the road. At that moment, all she could do was pray, asking the Lord for strength. He told her: 'Do not be afraid, for I am with you. They will not harm you.' As Lu watched, the wolves simply stared at her as she walked past. One by one, they left.

Another day, Lu went to pick tea leaves on a cliff over a deep, rocky valley. There wasn't anyone around. She slipped, but some branches protruding from the cliff stopped her fall and spared her life, knocking out eight of her teeth in the process. Her face bloodied from the impact, Lu fainted. After she awoke, she climbed back on the cliff and began limping to the camp, using a stick as a crutch. Her face was badly scraped and she had broken her arm. Because it was so late, everyone back in camp thought that Lu must have been killed. However, at midnight, Lu showed up and the people admitted that her God had once again saved her life. Slowly her wounds healed.

In 1979, after more than twenty years of hard labour at the prison farm, Lu wrote this poem:

As I look back on the path behind me,
It was full of ups and downs.
When I look forth into the future,
It will still be rough and bumpy.
However, only if I walk with the strength from
    God,
The roads ahead will be full of glory.
Seventy years of living is like a dream.
What is left is a useless body, all beaten-up.
It is so heartbreaking.
As I feel the pain in my heart, I am awake again.
I only see the righteous seeds of the gospel.
They are now bearing fruits and flowers.
I'll uplift my heart.
I'll press forward with my fragile feet.
I will not stop till I reach Paradise.
I will not pause even when I pass a resting place.
I just know that I have to fight to the end.
Until one day when I cannot even drag myself up,
    I know this is when one of my feet will have
    already stepped into Paradise.

The angels will surely lift me up.
As I open my eyes, I will see the merciful face of
my Lord.
My heart will fill with contentment beyond
words. Nothing can separate me from him.
There will be gold harps to accompany the choir.
Everlasting alleluia forever!

Lu was released from jail in 1979 as the government relaxed its control over religion. However,
there was no place for Lu to go to. She had no
family, no money and no home. A nurse, Sister
Yong, decided to take Madam Lu into her
home, despite her own heavy family burdens.
This was a beautiful testimony to all the neighbours. Sister Yong was later ordained and now
serves the Holy Trinity Church in Kunming.
Madam Lu, for her part, conducts a Bible study
every day, teaching and exhorting whoever
comes to her place, which is a gathering point
for Christian worship in a church-operated
retirement hostel.

Excuse me, Ma'am

by Marcus Oxley

Princess Diana had decided to support the 'Ban The Mine' campaign and visit Kuito, Angola . . . one of the most heavily mined cities in one of the most heavily mined countries in Africa.

I was working in Angola at the time as the country representative for the Irish aid agency Concern Worldwide. Along with several other NGO'S, Concern was working on the landmine problem. The Halo Trust were taking the landmines out of the ground, the Red Cross were giving people new plastic legs and arms, and Concern Worldwide was providing vocational training and small business skills to help people overcome their physical disabilities so they could earn a living and so be fully reintegrated back into their communities.

Anyway, as country rep I had to meet the plane at Kuito airport (where we were running the programme) and welcome Princess Diana off the plane. The princess arrived on a small plane and we were all introduced. After the official welcome and introductions, we were told by the British Ambassador we would have to wait at the airport until the next plane bringing the press photographers arrived. We all stood around, making small talk, both parties feeling a bit shy and hoping we wouldn't have to wait too long. I asked the Princess how her children were, explained the aim of the programme, how long we'd been there and things like that.

After about ten minutes, the Princess' bodyguard or escort came up to us and asked her to get ready for the press, as their plane was about to land. At this, Diana took a very small microphone and clipped it onto the inside collar of her white blouse. She had to pull out her blouse to thread the lead down inside and onto a small battery pack, which she placed down the back of her jeans. After a couple of minutes she had the job done, tucked in her blouse, tightened the belt on her jeans and, turning round to her butler on her left-hand side, looked down towards her bottom and asked him 'Does everything look all right?' – meaning were the shirt, battery and lead all tucked in well and not looking too cumbersome. I was stood immediately on the right-hand side of the princess, and in an unprompted reaction to her question, blurted out that 'Everything looked very well from my side!'

The Princess immediately started laughing, turned round and said to me 'Just remember who you're talking to!' It was a tongue in cheek comment that prompted a tongue in cheek reply, but it also suddenly occurred to me that I had just told the Princess Diana that she had a nice bottom . . . The team were in stitches, the Princess was smiling as only she could, I went very red and the Ambassador positively scowled at me.

The team and I (and I believe the princess too) all really enjoyed those few hours together in Kuito. Sadly, only a couple of months later, whilst we were all in Kuito, we watched the news of the tragic road accident in Paris in disbelief. I think those of us who she met in Angola will always have fond memories of our Princess.

Reclaiming the Outcast

by Janet Root

'Our family and most of our friends abandoned us when I tested positive for HIV,' says Jane, her low voice cracking with emotion. Jane's husband died several years ago from HIV/AIDS-related causes, leaving this young mother tormented by a consuming fear; that she will soon die and her children will have no place to live.

Never in Compassion's fifty-year history have we encountered a disaster with such devastating consequences for the world's children as the HIV/AIDS pandemic. AIDS is not only incurable, it also burdens its victims with the heavy baggage of social disgrace. In many places, the AIDS-infected are social pariahs, believed to be suffering the just consequences of their immoral behaviour. And in other corners of the world, casual contact with AIDS-affected families is avoided because of the fear of infection.

In short, the AIDS-infected and affected are today's social outcasts. And the innocent – the children – are paying an incalculable price. Many of the AIDS orphans in the world today are homeless and financially desperate. Nowhere is the plight of HIV/AIDS-affected children so visible, or the disease's stigma so palpable, as in sub-Saharan Africa. There, more than eleven million children have lost one or both parents to AIDS.

A Family's Shame

For Jane and her children, the shame surrounding HIV/AIDS is especially strong in Kikuyu, Kenya, where they live. Infection rates are believed to be as high as 30 per cent. Thankfully, church workers at the local Compassion-assisted Thigio Child Development Centre (CDC) came to the family's aid, registering Jane's sons James, aged five, and Paul, aged six, into the sponsorship programme. In addition to the regular Compassion support offered to the two boys, the family now receives nutritious food supplements to bolster their health, as well as needed medication and treatments, through Compassion's HIV/AIDS Fund.

AIDS education seminars held at the centre are designed to help parents overcome the shame associated with the disease and get the help they need. 'Some diseases are acceptable –

like malaria,' says Stephen Njoroge, a social
worker at the Thigio centre. 'AIDS isn't acceptable here, but Jane gained the courage to speak
up and tell us she was infected. HIV-positive
parents of the children in our programme are
also taught how to ensure that their children
will inherit their possessions, since stealing
property from children whose parents die from
AIDS is a big problem in Kenya.'

Most important, this family continues to
receive unconditional acceptance from the project staff workers – a powerful example of
Christ's love to this AIDS-ravaged community;
care that also reflects the tender compassion
Jesus demonstrated.

*Every Compassion programme in Africa offers
HIV/AIDS awareness training for children and
their parents. Classes are designed to help participants see beyond the disease's stigma and offer
Christ's compassion to its victims. HIV/AIDS pre-
vention, emphasising the biblical message of sexual
purity and faithfulness in marriage, is also taught.
This training programme serves as a model for
Compassion's programmes worldwide.*

It's the Condom Conundrum

by Peter Meadows

For western Christians, who tend to equate the condom with casual sex, the present global AIDS crisis poses a huge dilemma. To condom or not condom – that's the question. And, in answering it, Christians are not always being 'good news'.

So let's put the issue bluntly; should a Christian agency ever give out condoms? And, if so, in what circumstances?

But first, one indisputable fact. It's that, in the context of a programme of education and awareness raising, the distribution and correct use of condoms helps slow the spread of HIV in poor communities.

However, is it legitimate – in order to save lives – for Christians to encourage something that seems to endorse casual sex? Are there times when the lesser of two evils is the most Christian thing to do? And remember, we are not talking about western sophistication, where the evidence suggests that the more condoms you hand out the worse things can get. This is a very different picture. For example . . .

Meet Greeta – who, in a Zambian border town, sells her body night after night and day after day, with the truck drivers passing though as her eager customers.

Greeta's one of thousands who see this as the only way to keep their family from starvation. To her it's not a matter of choice but necessity. She isn't responsible for the fact that the crops have failed yet again. And there is no other work. But she does feel responsible for keeping her young family alive – in any way she can.

Tonight she will ply her trade – knowing that unprotected sex pays double. Will you give her a condom – with her future and that of her children in mind? Or take the moral high ground? Controversial as it sounds, the response of a Christian agency like World Vision is to teach women like this how to negotiate protected sex with their customers. And give them the condoms they need to do so.

And there are other settings that present equal challenges to our understanding of morality. For example, meet Jakob – who made a dreadful mistake while working away from home for six months and is now HIV positive and deeply remorseful. And meet Anna his wife. Will you leave them to their own devices? Or give them one of yours?

Meet Tabbi, Omoko and Lydia. One brutally raped by invading soldiers. One given unscreened blood when the delivery of her last child went wrong. The other, one of thousands waiting to hear the safe sex message that the overwhelmed and under-resourced community health workers in her area will one day have the time to patiently explain. What will you do for them on the condom front? Provide them?

For those who say that to do so 'sounds like saying sin is OK' the question has to be 'So what's your answer?' After all, isn't 'good news' supposed to be good news?

HIV/AIDS – the story in brief

The HIV epidemic is the most devastating that humanity has ever faced and has become the fourth biggest global killer.

- *Worldwide, more than 42 million people are living with AIDS and 20 million have already died.*
- *More than 14 million have become orphans having lost one or both their parents.*
- *There are an estimated 14,000 new cases of HIV/AIDS each day.*
- *Children under the age of fifteen make up 2,000 of the new daily cases of HIV/AIDS.*
- *Nearly 600,000 children under fifteen die each year from HIV/AIDS.*
- *In Swaziland, Botswana and some areas of South Africa, more than a third of pregnant women are HIV positive*
- *The virus will kill more people over the next 10 years than all the wars and disasters of the past fifty.*

In sub-Saharan Africa AIDS has wiped out fifty years of progress. Today, life expectancy is only forty-seven years. Without AIDS it would have been sixty-two years. And in some southern African countries up to half of all new mothers could die of AIDS.

Vive la Difference!

by Jeff Lucas

French was never my subject at school. My long-suffering French teacher, Mr Ernie Peckett (his real name, believe me), finally booted me out of the class because I got my French salutations wrong. I wanted to attract the attention of the spotty youth who sat at the desk in front of me. Instead of greeting him with a jaunty *'Bonjour Monsieur!'* I cut to the quick and jabbed him in the left buttock with a compass point. The wounded chap, not consoled by the fact that he had pierced flesh twenty years before it became fashionable, roared his protest in English, which signalled my final exit from the class.

So it is that I am now, like many English people, able to say *please* and *thank you* in French, and little more. Oh, I can also ask the time in French – but this is of little use, as I have my own watch. And I can ask for directions to the railway station – and knowing the way to *la gare* would have been helpful on a number of occasions – but I wouldn't be able to understand the reply, unless it involved some linguistically neutral pointing.

So I do what most English people do in France – I speak English with a French accent. '*Ello, ow arr yooo?*' I enquire, my tone a hybrid of Maurice Chevalier and Peter Sellers. I usu-ally tack a triumphant *Monsieur* on the end of every sentence, which is cool unless the person with whom I am conversing happens to be female. Thus, my trip to Paris this last week was a series of embarrassing gaffs with more arm waving than a windmill. I did try to ask for a chair in a café – but it turns out I that I actually asked to sit on a dog. Most Parisians I met smiled graciously when I apologised for my lack of French, and spoke fine English themselves.

One morning, I observed the antics of a herd of fellow English tourists – and felt ashamed. They were mimicking, in high-pitched parrot fashion, the Frenchman who was trying to sell them a Metro ticket. Obviously graduates from the Alf Garnett School of International Diplomacy, they were totally aghast – appalled even – because this gentleman didn't speak English like themselves, despite the screamingly obvious fact that they were guests in France – *his* country.

Quite simply, they were of the opinion that everyone should look and sound like they looked and sounded. Lurking beneath their crass behaviour was the deception that to be different is to be inferior. Kindly conform, or you are ever so slightly less valuable and significant than we are – for we, after all, are normal – or so the deception goes.

Religion often creates colourless uniformity. Those zealous bloodhounds, the religious leaders of the day, were always hot on the trail of Jesus. His main crime was that he was so *different*. They sniffed the scent of his uniqueness, and bayed like dogs. But, totally refusing to conform to *their* expectations, Jesus marched to a different drumbeat, one tapped out by his Father. At every turn, they tried to smother him with sameness, and desperately sought to buckle him into their religious straitjackets. They failed. Winsome escapologist that he was – and is – he not only resisted their cloning, but called his friends and followers to a life of studied non-conformity. He repeatedly spoke out about the bland pseudo-spirituality of the 'teachers of the law' in the Sermon on the Mount. His call? *'Don't be like them.'*

I am very guilty of religious control-freakery, being more comfortable around folks who worship like I do, who share a common view of how church leadership should be structured, and who use the same general charismatic vocabulary as my own. Perhaps that's normal – birds of a feather and all that – but when my desire for comfort causes me to be dismissive of others who don't fit the mould of my making, then blind arrogance has set in.

Sometimes parenting is about an inappropriate corralling of our children in an attempt to turn out little facsimiles of us. Here I blush: sometimes I have mistaken a desire that my children become more like Jesus with a crusade to actually make them like *me*. No letters needed, thanks, for pointing out the Grand Canyon-like gap between my Maker and me.

Incredibly, you and I can be guilty of demanding conformity of God himself. Church can be about a frantic attempt to make God fit our box. We frantically systemise him; try to peg him down like tiny people fussing over Gulliver. We, who are made in *his* image, desperately try to make him in *ours*.

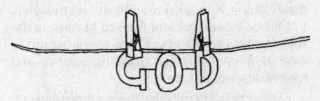

Let's build churches that are truly colourful and diverse communities, where eccentricity is welcomed rather than feared, and where God's one-offs don't need to sacrifice their uniqueness in order to belong. Regimen is for the cult, not the church.

And by the way, my French vocabulary has grown by 30 per cent . . . here's proof:

Au revoir.

Church with a Difference: Paraguay

by Stephen Rand

This was the countryside. Hundreds of miles from the nearest town, no electricity, no mod cons. We sat round the campfire and I sampled the barbecued raccoon. It was like being on safari in the wild west. As the sun went down, parakeets squawked and flocked to roost in the line of grapefruit trees. There was a sound, a sort of deep clanging, clunking sound, and everyone started to move.

They were responding to the ringing of the church bell. About fifty metres through the trees we came upon the Anglican church. The church bell was a short piece of railway line hanging from a tree and being banged with a stick. (Railway line? Just where was the nearest railway line?) The roof was the clear night sky, with more stars than I had ever seen, and the Milky Way revealed as if a paintbrush had daubed the heavens. The walls were the trees of the forest. At first I thought people were approaching with torches, then I realised that fireflies were flickering through the trees. In short, I thought it was the most beautiful church I had ever seen. I still do. I have since stood in giant cathedrals and gazed in awe at the lofty pillars and the fan vaulting, then I have remembered that these are human attempts to replicate the creator's woodwork.

But in the end the church is people. The small Indian community gathered, and sat on the log benches that were arranged two-deep in a simple square. Then the old Indian pastor, the first baby born in the settlement after the missionaries had built Makthlawaiya, way back in 1907, stood at the lectern – a branch set as a crossbar on two branch uprights – and flicked on a tiny Duracell battery torch to read the scripture. 'In my Father's house there are many mansions . . .' he read from John 14. It seemed deeply appropriate.

As We Are Fully Known . . .

by Philip Yancey

Early in my marriage I would haltingly reveal secrets about myself to my wife, secrets I had never told anyone. 'Do you still love me?' I would ask. 'Yes,' she would assure me, even when the secrets may have caused her pain. I learned from her a truth I would later understand about God: only if you are fully known can you be fully loved.

My spiritual growth has meant bringing a succession of secrets, in fear and trembling, to God, only to find that God of course knew the secret all along, and loved me anyhow. I have learned that God is hardly surprised by my failure. Knowing me better than I know myself, God expects failure from me. I am more sinful than I ever imagined – and also more loved by God.

Into Africa . . .

by Emma Stratton

Having been briefed up to the eyeballs and prayed out of the door by the UK based team at the Tearfund offices in Teddington, it was with much poorly concealed excitement that I rattled through my goodbyes. In all of the build-up to leaving the UK, I didn't get bothered by the responsibility of co-ordinating the distribution of seeds and tools to ten thousand families in one of the most remote, geographically inhospitable, war-torn regions of the world. Even the sobering practicality of writing a will did little to quash my zeal. It was all too big an adventure to get spooked by. It was as though in my naïve enthusiasm, another gear of living had been found. This was what I had impatiently waited for, the chance to get out there and get on with 'it'.

I took off from Heathrow on February 8, 1999. With the prospect of eight hours or so on board, I made the most of the on-board services provided. I sprawled out on four unused seats, cocooned myself in all four blankets, headphones on, donned an eye-mask, and was particularly delighted by the royal blue and cerise towelling sockettes that may still, to this day, be hot-footing around southern Sudan.

Another Tearfund 'rookie' (Phil) and I hotelled a short distance from the Nairobi office for the first few nights. A whole room to myself – surely the height of international travel! We went down to the restaurant for dinner, and were somewhat perturbed by the fact that when we returned, both our rooms had been broken into and our stuff rifled through. Perhaps broken into is the wrong phrase – there was no sign of a forced entry. An inside job? Phil had had some money stolen, but that was it. Though relieved, I did feel strangely offended that the criminal did not deem any of my possessions worth nicking. The money was not recovered, but a man walking around the hotel grounds later that night was severely beaten by the police in spite of the total lack of evidence linking him to the crime.

Tearfund's southern Sudan programme

Following its inception in 1998, this was increasing in size at the start of 1999. Along with half a dozen other new team members recruited from Nairobi, our first few days were based in the city for orientation and induction. My desire to get into Sudan had become a growing itch, but towards the end of the orientation came the bad news that the security situation in Mike Kilo was poor, and therefore it would not be possible to fly in for a few days.

However, we were able to drive a brand spanking new vehicle up the backbone of Kenya through the Rift Valley to Lokichokio where it was to be flown out to our project site, a two-day trip. Rob and I shared the drive. He was my project co-ordinator, my boss. By the time we got to Loki we were getting on well enough for him not to fulfil his threat of putting me 'on the next flight out'. The drive was phenomenal, spectacular scenery, minimal traffic, beautiful weather.

The majority of relief programmes in southern Sudan are operated out of Nairobi. Strategy co-ordination meetings are held there; the UN, programme-funding donors and other NGOs (non-governmental organisations – like Tearfund) are all represented there. Lokichokio, a Turkana town on the Kenyan-Sudanese border is next, the logistics base; a three-hour flight or two-day drive from Nairobi. In 1999 almost everyone and everything relief-related entering or leaving southern Sudan from Kenya went through Loki, transient home to the assortment of 'Mercenaries, Misfits, Madmen and Missionaries' that choose to stay, for their honourable and less honourable motives, in disaster-riddled, war-torn places.

Loki was the entrance and exit point for relief workers going into Sudan (the field). After six or so weeks of work, rest and recuperation was taken (R&R). Relief workers were flown down to Nairobi to relax in Kenya. It's not easy in Nairobi; but the coast, the lakes, safari parks – it's quite hard not to relax in a country of such beauty. Then back up to Loki, and the cycle began again. Loki was the last place to access tapped water, air-conditioning, cold beer or cold anything, chairs with cushions on or telephones. Part hub of a well-established, multi-million dollar relief operation, part MASH-style camp, part prison with its perimeter fencing and security, part den of iniquity – Loki was a place of many faces.

Like many of the Loki offices, Tearfund's was a large converted container, with one window, two doors, a large identifying Tearfund sticker and a hammock outside for the daily siestas. Furnishings totalled a couple of desks, four chairs, a big book case, a laptop, paper trays and files galore, wall maps riddled with allegedly strategically based pins, a satellite telephone, numerous GP300 handsets for short distance radio communications, and a high-frequency (HF) radio set for talking with Nairobi and the different project sites in Sudan.

Sudan is a country at war with itself. Since 1955 there has only been peace for one decade. It boasts, with little pride, a speculated greater number of human casualties than the combined death toll of the Rwandan and Chechnyan conflicts. Since 1983, two million people have died because of the war, and four million have had to move from their homes. A massive 92 per cent of the population live below the internationally recognised poverty line.

The war rolls on, the south wanting independence from the north. The stakes have been massively exacerbated in recent years with the discovery of rich oil fields. The north versus south picture, though, is too simplistic. Within the south are many tribal groups, with a bloody history of inter-tribal fighting for power, control and land rights.

The relief effort operates in an active war zone. Safety and security of relief workers are high on the agenda. Plans and procedures for 'what to do if . . .' are written up, drilled into people, updated, implemented and revised. For the majority of NGOs, the UN has responsibility to inform and arrange the evacuation of personnel when judged appropriate. It all sounds exhilarating, but the disruption to local relationships and project work is massive, not to mention the stress of living with the constant threats of danger.

In February, the dry season, Sudan was brown. A GAP khaki brown, with occasional bursts of green tree canopies, randomly scattered. River beds meandered casually along their lazy courses, so casually they were dry; river beds without the river. And it was flat, contourless, a doddle for an Ordnance Survey cartographer! The flight from Loki into Malualkon, our destination, took three hours. Known affectionately to all as Mike Kilo, it is in the county of Aweil East, home to the Dinka tribe, tall, lean, dignified pastoralists.

As the plane approached the air strip, it circled the Dinka village; mud huts with grass roofs, a water pump crowded with women in bright coloured wraps, a few large fenced-off compounds of a number of huts. Rob pointed out the landmarks; the Tearfund compound of tents, mud huts and its long distinctive stores, a few narrow tracks crisscrossing, and a long straight dirt road built by the Brits in the 1950s, stretching from east to west.

The plane was met by a large crowd. One guy had a wheelbarrow and our bags were trundled off to the compound. There was so much, too much to try and take in – how black the people were, how many smiling faces, the heat, the naked children touching your arm whilst you walked to see if the 'white' would rub off, the heat, the welcoming speechettes of various local dignitaries, the heat, the stares, the unfamiliar language, the heat, not knowing where anything was or how to get anywhere. I grinned inanely, shook hands repeatedly, stuck close to Rob and the others from the plane, and grinned some more.

Tearfund Mike Kilo

We walked the five minutes through the village to the compound, into something of an oasis of tranquillity. Inside only the Tearfund team, staff and invited guests had access – our place. It was divided into three sections:

- ◆ Outer – the stores, where kit and equipment and oil, sugar, unimix (the high energy, nutritious soya based mix that we distributed in the feeding programme) etc. were stored – the items necessary for the project to operate.
- ◆ Middle – the office, team food store, vehicle parking and team eating area. Only team members and local staff involved directly with these areas were allowed in this section.
- ◆ Inner – the team's sleeping quarters, loo and shower block. The team only area.

The immediate striking feature was the tree. It must have been the biggest in Mike Kilo. One of the churches used to meet under it but offered Tearfund its shade and the immediate surrounding area on which to build the compound. It served as a landmark in my early days. It could be seen from much of the village and many were the times I appreciated its shade. February was the height of the dry season; we reached fifty-two degrees Celsius one day! In that kind of temperature your body just clamours to stop. The Sudan sun at its hottest is a real enemy. I have a sun-loving reputation developed through summers running around naked on the beach (predominantly during my infant years!), but I quickly started slapping on the cream, covering up with loose cottons and planning my routes around the village with maximal tree cover and minimal mileage.

Our mud-walled, thatched-roofed homes were called tuckles. I was in a tent, though, whilst I was there. The interior furnishings were a goat-skin strung bed and accompanying mozzy net, some shelves for clothes, a small table and – depending on your status within the team – a chair or a foot stool. My foot stool was small. Such simple living, a rucksack worth of personal kit, was great.

The Tearfund team consisted of a Ugandan nutritionist, an Ethiopian community health educator, two Kenyan nurses, a Brit compound manager, a Sudanese food security officer, a Brit project co-ordinator, and me with the auspicious title of 'seeds and tools logistician'. There were also over twenty Sudanese staff, feeding assistants, water carriers, educators, compound workers, drivers, cooks and cleaners. Some spoke English, others did not and my Dinka linguistic skills were poor. However, we can communicate and understand one another a lot more than I'd realised without words. Some of my favourite 'conversations' involved mime skills that have enhanced my Christmas charade ability massively.

+ Two arms outstretched from the shoulders accompanied by a mechanical humming noise – an aeroplane.
+ One arm held out in front of me, the other arm jumping over the top of it – tomorrow.
+ Either arm held at a considered angle in the sky – indicative of the position of the sun – time of day.
+ Pretending to receive a package from someone – the mail pouch from the pilot.
+ Put it all together – a request to pick up the mail pouch from the incoming flight ETA 'whatever' time tomorrow.

Admittedly there is room for error in all that, and it was relatively time consuming – but it was good fun.

* * * *

The project had been set up in October 1998 in response to the high rates of malnutrition in the area and had a three-pronged approach to its work. The medical vulnerability of the elderly and the young to disease and malnourishment is intensified within the Sudanese culture. It is the man of the house who gets first shout on food, therefore younger children are particularly vulnerable to the effects of food deficits. The immediate feeding needs of under-fives were met by weekly targeted distributions from supplementary feeding centres in six different locations throughout the county. Poor health practices augmented the effects of food shortages; for example, drinking unclean water could induce diarrhoea. Teams of local health educators would encourage communities to adopt less risky behaviours, such as filtering water or not using stagnant ponds.

Food security aims to provide a more medium term solution to situations of food shortages, to 'feed for life by teaching fishing, rather than feeding for a day by giving fish.' In the project this included the distribution of fishing kits, education in crop growing, and the seeds and tool distribution, which is where my work fitted in. The time pressure was to get the distributions completed in time for the planting season, to allow sowing to occur at about the time of the first rains. Too soon, and the seeds might be eaten by recipients to meet their immediate hunger needs; too late, and it might not be possible for the planes freighting in the seeds and tools to land because of a boggy airstrip. It was tricky to predict the exact dates with any accuracy. The cows in Mike Kilo were lying down and standing up sporadically with seemingly no regard to the fact that they were one of my primary meteorological forecasting tools.

Another issue affecting timing was security. The last thing we wanted was the compound sitting full of seeds and tools if there was the possibility we'd have to evacuate before completing the distribution. They were valuable commodities, especially in the quantity that we had on board. The middle section of the compound was at one stage well carpeted with two hundred rows' worth of fifty sacks of packages. Relationships with the community were really good, but having that quantity of items, both in terms of economic and immense practical value, sitting inside our grass fence perimeter could have put an awful lot of temptation into the equation.

* * * *

The insecurity that had postponed our arrival in Mike Kilo had passed. Warawar, a village to our north, bore the scars. Part had been torched during an attack – torching a mud hut with a dried grass roof leaves a predictable outcome. The first afternoon we arrived, Rob wanted to talk with the local leaders and see if any assistance was necessary. I was overwhelmed by the heat, the apparent lack of road and trepidation over what we'd see at the village.

Alison was next to me – Tearfund's community health education co-ordinator. She'd been with the programme for six months and I was floored by how relaxed she seemed. As though six squashed people bouncing along in a 4x4 listening to a language you didn't understand in sweltering heat in the middle of nowhere heading towards a village that had been burning a few days ago was the most normal thing in the world. Als was in Mike Kilo for all of my first week before heading off elsewhere. She was a real support, managing to strike a balance of introducing, telling and showing, and letting me learn by myself.

Driving into Warawar, it was immediately evident which part of the village had suffered. The mud huts were now just charred walls. They were close together so the fire must have easily danced from one hut to the next. Although the fire was just days ago, people were already rebuilding. Some just needed to re-roof, while other huts were so damaged that total reconstruction was necessary. I was struck by the reaction of many. Rather than anger or mournful resignation, there seemed to be an incredible sense of pragmatic acceptance. In Sudan, it happens, in what is already a climatically inhospitable land where a war has raged for years. There's a big difference between resignation – being beaten by it, and acceptance – acknowledging that that is how it is, but getting on with it as best you can. A whole generation has grown up knowing only war in southern Sudan and have seen little sign of imminent peace, yet life goes on.

Ethiopia '85 provided the first pictures of hungry people I remember seeing. I enthusiastically joined Bob Geldof's Run the World, lolloping along the Jersey coastline with the crowds. I watched the six o'clock news by myself one night with tears coursing down my cheeks. My reaction in Sudan, though, was starkly different. I remember feeling incredibly concerned and guilty over my lack of emotion. Hard-hearted? Maybe. A coping strategy? Probably.

As part of my orientation to the project, in my first week I visited a couple of the supplementary feeding centre sites. Saturday was Mike Kilo's day. The children brought to the centre were weighed and measured, and given a medical check on their health from the project nurses. Questions were asked about food availability, eating habits and diarrhoea, with a view to minimising further bouts of illness and exploring possibilities of accessing other food sources. If the child was ill, they would be referred to the local primary health care clinic run by another Mike Kilo based NGO. If, for a number of weeks, the child had consistently maintained their weight at the target level for their height, they would be discharged from the feeding programme, or, if according to weight for height standards – or other nutritional indicators – they were assessed as being malnourished, they would be admitted to the feeding programme, given an identity bracelet and number and issued with a week's worth portion of unimix to be made into porridge. They would have some time with the nurses encouraging positive nutritional practices, and be asked to revisit next week.

One of the ways I coped with the daily scenes of suffering around us was to rationalise situations; a kind of logical detachment from sentimentality. There aren't many vents for it in that kind of environment. At home, after a bad day at work, I'd have walked the beach, called a friend, belted a squash ball round a court. In Sudan, if you walk, you're accompanied by children. Your friends are your team mates, coping with similar stuff in their own ways. The best you could do was jog with that same posse of giggling children at your heels daring one another to try and touch you.

I had to develop a new repertoire of coping skills – one was this rationalisation of situations; another, a commitment to work at what was within my sphere of control – to get on with my bit, and accept that which I couldn't change. I learnt to write as well. Originally, I thought I was doing it to keep people at home in touch. But I found that putting on paper the events, and to a lesser extent my attached thoughts and to a still lesser extent, my feelings, acted as a real cathartic release for me. I love being heard in my friendships. Conversation is great, but with some things, I don't need or want people to respond. I simply want to be heard and, in the absence of verbal communication, writing was my only way of knowing that I would be.

* * * *

'Echo Sierra what is your position, over?'

'Just leaving Whisky Romeo heading for Mike Kilo, ETA twenty-five minutes.'

'Hold your position until further notice, copy that?'

'Copy.'

I still remember the conversation, detecting the edge of urgency and concern in Rob's voice; still remember the tangible surge of adrenaline and involuntary acceleration of my heart rate. In spite of being with a driver, a local counterpart security man and the vehicle being surrounded by a crowd, I felt utterly and absolutely alone.

It was probably only about fifteen minutes, but my brain went into overdrive. Insecurity. I had heard about it, done some training, been held up at 'gun point' by enthusiastic balaclavaed volunteers during training, heard the tales of various incidents that had become folklore. There seemed to me to be an air of stripe earning about the whole thing. Until now, I had had an almost romantic image of fleeing from a pursuing enemy, and naturally, in my mind, the stories always ended up happily ever after.

The security threats in Sudan at the time were mainly ground based. Mike Kilo was in rebel-held territory 'governed' by the SPLA, the Sudanese Peoples Liberation Army, I always felt rebel was a bit strong, but it was non-government aligned. The government of Sudan (GoS) therefore would at times launch major ground-based offensives to claim back various towns in the south. A train would pass along the track forty kilometres to the west of Mike Kilo, from north to south, throughout the dry season carrying weapons, supplies and soldiers to bolster the handful of government-held towns and garrisons in the south. The train was accompanied by government soldiers but also by the PDF (People's Defence Force), often on horseback. Naturally, the train was a target for the SPLA. On its return journey north, the empty train would allegedly carry plunder from villages that troops had attacked. These villages tended to be within a relatively narrow corridor near to the railway that Mike Kilo was generally beyond. Invariably, therefore, fighting and tension were constant when the train was on the move.

Tension had been high in Mike Kilo for the last few days. Longer serving team members were aware that the community seemed nervous. Rumours of potential invasion were rife and although of little substance, were never quite substance-less enough to ignore. Many villagers had packed their few possessions and the staff frequently nipped out of the compound to check on family members and stay abreast with news. Security procedures were tightened up, radio checks with Loki became more frequent, regular information-sharing meeting with other NGOs started, our 'quick run' back packs of various useful items and supplies necessary for sustaining life in the event of an emergency evacuation rarely left our sides. Mine was more substantial than most – alongside my compass, map, water bottle, purification tablets, first aid kit, food and spare radio battery went a few of what I felt to be 'essential luxury' items – chewing gum, deodorant, my photo album and a good book. I was thinking quality of life, as opposed to just life!

It was during my second week in Sudan, and I was on my way back from a village to the north when the instruction to hold my position came. Tearfund have a security plan in each location detailing potential risks, preventative measures, safety procedures and evacuation plans. I'd read it twice, but during those minutes holding my position in Warawar, knowing something was awry in Mike Kilo, yet clueless to the details, I made a mental note to re-reread the information asap. I mentally ran through the location of the 'quick run points' (places identified 1-2km from our compound to quickly run to if necessary). I stared at the radio microphone, finger poised on the button, wondering what was going on at base. Why hadn't Rob called back? Had they had to evacuate? Had anyone picked up any of my stuff? Eventually an incoming call rang through.

'Proceed to base directly.'

Having found our driver in the market, who had nipped off to get a couple of mangos (they were on special apparently), we proceeded very directly, managing to knock about a quarter off the usual journey time.

By the time we arrived back in Mike Kilo, the fever pitch had dropped. Rob relayed to me over a stiff mug of tepid water how the staff had fled the compound whilst telling members of the expat team to do likewise – the village was under attack. Villagers were running into the bush, bundles on heads, children scooped up, homes abandoned. The team prepared for an immediate overland evacuation, which is when Rob first called me on the radio.

It transpired that the trigger to this was a pack of wild dogs, rather than marauding assailants on horseback. The dogs ran through the village, pursued vigorously by a group of

stone-throwing boys. Villagers saw the boys
running and immediately assumed the enemy
were at hand. They ran. Our staff understand-
ably did likewise, and so on. That is the ongoing stress that the southern Sudanese of that
area (and others) are living under.

It had been my first taste of the fear of insecurity – and the excitement; the fear of being in
a situation over which I had so little control. I
could follow the security plan and get to the
right place to meet the team, but I think it was
this incident that brought home to me the fact
that I was indeed a stranger in a strange land at
war, where I didn't really understand the rules
of daily living.

* * * *

Rob's contract and time in Mike Kilo finished in
March. I am amazed at the phenomenal rate
that friendships and trust develop when you
work, rest and play 'team'. In just that month,
I'd grown not only to respect Rob as my manager, but really to enjoy the times we spent
together as friends. I wasn't looking forward to
him going, and I therefore wasn't looking forward to his replacement arriving – but she did.

Rob had a week to hand over to George, and
during that time you could see him winding
down. The day Rob left, the whole team bun-
dled down to the airstrip in the back of the

pick-up to wait for his plane. It was late, and a really hot day. I took myself off quietly and sat on a tree, and thought, prayed and watched. It was ridiculous, I'd only known this guy for one month and yet was finding the prospect of watching him leave harder than some of the goodbyes I'd done in the UK. I think trust was a big part of it. On a few occasions of insecurity I'd really had to trust Rob – his judgement, his leadership, his decision-making. With him leaving, I had to redevelop that trust from scratch in George.

The plane eventually circled lazily before trundling down the airstrip towards us. Goodbyes were said in the noisy dust and heat as the propellers whirred, and he was gone. I got back to the compound, George asked me a question about something or other, and I just burst in tears, quite an uncharacteristic response. The average length of contract with DRT is six to eight months. You get to say goodbye to a lot of colleagues and friends. You also get to meet a lot of new colleagues and potential friends.

The pain of saying goodbye to Rob was eased markedly by the speed that George and I became buddies. Once again, it was friendship at an accelerated rate. One of the best things about my time with Tearfund has been the friends I have been fortunate enough to make along the way. A very special bond of shared experience links people and, in many cases, holds a long way down the line.

Please Sir, Can I Have Some More?

by Keith Danby

I have to confess to having a distinct dislike of Indian food. Nor do I care much for the in-flight food on most airlines. Put them them together and you have quite a combination, as I was to discover on a Jet Airways flight from Hyderabad to Delhi. I was travelling with two good friends, Peter Maiden and Tony Sargent, who seemed to have asbestos stomachs.

As the cabin crew started to serve the in-flight meal, I realised I had not eaten since my banana at breakfast and my stomach began to grumble! However, one look at the curry that was being enthusiastically received by my friends immediately put me off any notion of hunger. I took the tray anyway, minus the curry and my eyes lit up as I saw the bread roll and the chocolate biscuit.

The roll was great and as the pretty Jet Airways stewardess passed by, I caught her eye, smiled nicely and politely asked would it be possible to have another roll. She smiled sweetly, shook her head and promptly went to find me a roll. Moments later she returned with it.

I ate the roll and then the chocolate biscuit. The same sweet lady passed by and again I caught her eye and this time I smile and asked would it be possible for her to find me another chocolate biscuit. Once again she smiled sweetly, shook her head and hurried down to the galley. Again she promptly returned with my extra biscuit.

I settled back feeling satisfied and comfortable. The meal trays were efficiently cleared away and the crew started to hand out hot towels to freshen up after the meal. Once again the pretty hostess served our row. She handed Tony a hot towel and Peter a hot towel and then looked at me, smiled sweetly and handed me two hot towels!

Resilient People Find Meaning and Purpose in the Storm

by John Ortberg

Victor Frankl was a Viennese psychiatrist who survived the Nazi death camps at Auschwitz and Treblinka. He discovered that the imprisoned person who no longer had a goal was unlikely to survive. His work led him to the conclusion that what he titled 'Man's Search for Meaning' was in fact the primary force in life.

We who lived in concentration camps can remember the men who walked through the huts comforting others, giving away their last piece of bread. They may have been few in number, but they offer sufficient proof that everything can be taken away from a man but one thing: the last of the human freedoms – to choose one's attitude in any given set of circumstances, to choose one's way. The way in which a man accepts his fate and all the suffering that it entails, the way in which he takes up his cross, gives him ample opportunity – even in the most difficult circumstances – to add a deeper meaning to his life.

'Let the Little Children Come'

by Paul O'Rourke

Single mothers with babies strapped to their backs work for a pittance in the endless coffee plantations of Kenya's central province of Ndumberi. Many of the mothers and children are malnourished, and at risk of poisoning from the insecticides used on local crops. Often children don't survive their tender first years in these harsh conditions. Those that do find it hard to get jobs and end up as street children or prostitutes in the capital, Nairobi, about 25km away. Illiteracy is high and alcoholism and drug abuse is rife.

It is here in the midst of the squalor and despair that a local church, Ndumberi All Nations Gospel Church, in partnership with Compassion, is helping the families most at risk. The church's early childhood development programme targets pregnant mothers and those with newborns to five year olds. For seven years, the church has been providing food, health care, counselling, vocational courses, health and hygiene training, literacy courses,

Christian teaching and prayer and emotional support to hundreds of mothers and babies.

'We have seen a great change, not just in the families, but in the community,' says project social worker Janet Njuguna. 'When they first came, they were severely malnourished and suffered from many other ailments. They did not have a hope. Many were lost in the first few years of life. But now, they are well fed, confident and happy.'

Janet says the Compassion programmes had given the church access to the local community. 'We have the goodwill of the community and the other agencies with whom we network. It has brought light into the village in a great, great way and changed the children and families' eternal destiny.'

Families attend the centre five days a week. There is a nursery for babies while older children are separated into classes, where they learn through play, songs, drama and stories. A resident nurse provides basic health care and first aid, and an army of volunteers provides meals and supervision.

Mothers come in the afternoon after work and are offered counselling, food, literacy training, Bible studies, vocational programmes and instruction in health and hygiene. Most of the mothers are single teenagers who have had poor role models as parents.

Children graduate from the Meals Plus programme to Compassion's learning-for-life programme where they are individually sponsored. Sponsorship meets their educational needs, provides health care, counselling, Christian teaching and social skills. In all, more than 350 children are being cared for through the two programmes.

Compassion Kenya Meals Plus coordinator Catherine Mbotela says the church was not taking over the parenting role. 'We are just the facilitators. Parents have to face up to the responsibility of parenting. This is their project and their children.'

Senior Pastor Peter Nimemia says: 'Poverty can only ever be broken when people are givers, not takers.' He proudly looked at the throng of children and declares: 'These children are the church of today.'

Meeting Mother Theresa

by Stephen Rand

The immediate impression was just how tiny and frail she appeared, an impression quickly supplemented by the realisation of the animation and humour of her conversation. When she discovered we were from England she expressed her delight at the news that Malcolm Muggeridge – 'dear Malcolm' – had finally joined the Roman Catholic church, news that had only broken that morning. She graciously accepted our gift of a Tearfund calendar for the coming year, which featured photographs that Tony had taken on previous overseas visits. 'I like this,' she said, 'your pictures give dignity back to the poor.' Garth gave her one of his cassettes and, with a twinkle in her eye, she explained that she was terribly sorry that she could not ask him to sing, but the sisters had taken a vow of silence for the day.

There seemed to be a potential logical gap in this reasoning, but my ego had not yet reached the point where I felt I could or should challenge Mother Teresa's powers of rational thinking. Rather, I found myself playing the part of 'man impressed by being in presence of celebrity': Tony took my picture with her (who knows, one day it might be useful to include in a book and make me look important) and I asked her to sign Susan's Bible – a pocket one I used on overseas visits. 'Be holy, for Jesus who loves you is holy,' she wrote.

After forty minutes the audience was over. She had been completely unassuming and completely at ease, even though she must have known that we were doing little more than regarding her as one of the sights of Calcutta. And of course I plead guilty to the charge of name-dropping. It's amazing how much mileage one can make out of forty minutes. I am not sure I can claim any justification from the fact that others, some world-famous in their own right, have done the same. I have even made a half-hearted attempt to collect other signatures in my Bible, Christians who have impressed me but whose names will not impress others.

The saving grace is this: Mother Teresa became the most famous Christian in the world, and she became famous for caring for the poor. Her celebrity status was founded on genuine worth, her fame earned by a lifetime of service. Vijayan Pavamani said to me later that day 'Because of Mother Teresa, everyone in India associates Christianity with care for the poor.' What an epitaph. One billion people left with a Christ-like impression of Christ. The photo Tony took that day is a treasured possession; there is a radiant inner beauty that transcends the wrinkles of age.

So when I have dropped her name, I hope that occasionally I have at least encouraged others to reflect on the basis of her fame, and what it really means to be a follower of Jesus. As Tony Campolo memorably put it in a Tearfund video I produced: 'They gave Mother Teresa a Nobel prize for doing what every Christian is supposed to do.'

All We Like Sheep

by Philip Yancey

My wife and I stayed once in a bed and break-fast in rural Tasmania, the rugged island off the southern coast of Australia. A sheep rancher had built a guest cottage in the middle of his fields, and for an extra fee lodgers could take a meal in the ranch house. Aware that we would probably never eat fresher lamb, we signed on.

Over dinner I innocently asked about the odd colouring – orange, red, blue and green blotches – we had seen on the rumps of his sheep. 'Ah, that's how we tell when the ewes mated,' he explained with a chuckle. 'I hang a container of coloured chalk in a rather strategic place on my ram. He leaves his mark when he does his duty, and that way I know that all the ewes with orange rumps, say, were serviced on the twenty-first. When the due date rolls around – sheep are almost always fertile, you see, and they deliver right on schedule – I can herd the orange ewes into the barn and give them special care.'

In the next few minutes I learned much more about the reproductive habits of sheep. Each ewe has only a six-hour window of receptivity to mating. This poses no problem to the ram, who can infallibly sense which ewe might welcome him at any given moment. The rancher relied on ten rams to 'service' four thousand female sheep, which meant that the rams worked themselves to exhaustion over several weeks, losing much of their body weight in the process. All work, no romance. When I saw a scrawny, bedraggled ram, his chores done, his strength dissipated, good for nothing but the slaughterhouse and even then unfit for human consumption, I breathed a prayer of thanks for human sexual arrangements. (Zoologists note that very few species – humans, dolphins, some primates, and the large cats – engage in sex as a form of pleasure.)

The next morning as I went jogging through the fields, taking care where I stepped, I tried to imagine life from the sheep's point of view. Ninety per cent of waking hours they spend wandering around, heads down, looking for lush green grass. Every so often a pesky dog barks and nips at their heels, and to humour him and shut him up they move in the direction he wants. Lo, better grass often awaits them there. As weather changes, they learn to huddle together against the rain and wind.

Once a year a rambunctious cousin appears among them and dashes from sheep to sheep, leaving the ewes marked with strange colours on their rumps. Bellies swell, lambs emerge, and attention turns to weaning these small, frisky creatures and watching them gambol through the grass. Brothers and sisters may disappear, sometimes attacked by a Tasmanian devil – these carnivorous marsupials, nastier than any cartoon stereotype, really do exist! – and sometimes ushered away by the two-legged one. The same upright creature periodically drives them into a barn where he shaves off their coats, leaving them cold and embarrassed (sheepish) for a time.

As I jogged, it occurred to me that sheep, to the degree they think at all, may well presume they order their own destiny. They chew cud, roam the fields, make choices, and live out their lot with only a few rude interruptions from dogs, devils, rams and humans. Little do they know that the entire scenario, from birth to death and every stage in between, is being orchestrated according to a rational plan by the humans who live in the ranch house.

C.S. Lewis conjectured, 'There may be Natures piled upon Natures, each supernatural to the one beneath it.' Do we stand in relation to God, as sheep stand in relation to us? The Bible suggests that in some ways we do. 'It is (God) who made us, and we are his; we are his people, the sheep of his pasture,' wrote a psalmist. Note the possessives: *his* people, *his* pasture. According to this point of view, we live out our days in a world owned by another. We may insist on autonomy – 'We all, like sheep, have gone astray' – but in the end that autonomy is no more impressive, or effective, than the autonomy of a Tasmanian ewe.

If God exists, and if our planet represents God's work of art, we will never grasp why we are here without taking that reality into account.

When Seeing Really is Believing

by Peter Meadows

The place, a rural – and I do mean 'rural' – village in Cambodia. With drought for half the year and floods for the other. Where to be hungry is normal, education is sparse and life fragile, particularly for those under five.

The setting – a 'deck' open to the elements but for its wooden roof, and set on stilts ready for the rains that will eventually come. The audience – me, with about sixty sponsored children at my feet looking on. The occasion – the members of the Village Development Committee presenting me with a report of their gradual emergence from poverty. And it was here seeing truly became believing.

In my head was all the theory about changing the future of poor communities. That creating lasting development – the jargon is 'sustainable' – has to involve giving genuine ownership to those whose lives are to be transformed. That *they* are those who must do the work – evaluating *their* own need, setting *their* own priorities and being the real change-makers. This was the theory and now it was coming to life before my own eyes.

With the help of huge sheets of paper I received an amazing conducted tour of what is, what needs to be and what this most needy group of people are doing to bridge the gap. It was all their own work, thanks to the highly skilled input of a specialist Community Development Worker and their team.

With the help of a range of PLAs – that's Participatory Learning Activities to the uninitiated – they'd been given the help to create a map showing the 'streets' and 'landmarks' of the patch they called 'home'. With the same kind of help they had also drawn up an inventory of what they had – the people, ranked by age and level of poverty; the houses, even including what they were made of; the animals, all counted down to the last chicken; and much more.

And with more of the same help they'd also created an amazing and highly sophisticated assessment of their village's needs. They talked me through the contents of a large flipchart and animatedly they explained what the real issues were and why. Which impacted the other. Where they had needed to act first.

Next they itemised came the help they'd been given to change their future – things they had no way of providing themselves. The quantity of high-grade rice seed down to the last kilo. The number of chickens, pigs and other livestock received on loan – to be repaid when the breeding season was over. The number of wells and pumps provided. And so on and so on and so on.

Here were people who, probably only two or three years earlier, had been bowed down by their circumstances with no road map for the future. Now I was looking at a group of barely educated and somewhat unsophisticated people who had it more together than many small business in the west. They had a vision, a plan, a budget – and were getting the skills training and additional resources to make lasting change a reality.

Before my eyes was a group for whom life had once been hopeless beyond words. Yet now I could see that they were facing their future with confidence. I'd seen the theory put into practice – but I'd seen even more. Because now, forever etched in my mind, is the vision of the proud and positive faces of the committee and the wide eyes of the sponsored children.

Seeing is believing and I can only ask 'One day, won't all development look like this?' I'd like to believe it will.

Clean and safe water

- 1.3 billion people have no access to clean water.

- In the developing world contaminated water accounts for 80 per cent of all disease.
- Contaminated water claims the lives of five million children a year.

Every day 1.3 billion people lack the twenty-five litres of water needed for drinking, sanitation and food preparation in order to survive; while the average UK citizen uses 150–200 litres for things like showering, bathing, laundry, drinking, cooking, cleaning, gardening and car washing.

Set Off and See!

by Hilary Price

Someone has said, 'Attempt great things for God, expect great things of God.' How many of us attempt even tiny things? How many of us set out into each day with no real expectation of God being remotely interested in our little lives and therefore not even considering that he may be interested in the lives of those who also populate our day? I have found, in my own life, that when I set off with a prayerful sense of expectation then I go through the day with anticipation and usually it is not disappointed.

Recently I flew to England for a short holiday and then back to Canada. When I arrived at check-in, for the outward leg of my journey, to my horror I discovered, with a little help from the girl at the desk, that my tickets were all for the date of the day before. I had come a day late and missed all my flights!! 'It is Easter and all the legs of your journey are overbooked. You can probably get from here to Chicago, but you may then have to wait three days for a connection to England,' she told me. I looked at my husband who, I have to say at this point, was gasping for air like a goldfish out of water and who, for one of the few times since I have know him, was at a loss for words! I looked at my daughter, who simply said, 'How could this happen?' and burst into tears. I won't dwell on who had booked the tickets, but I did find myself asking the same question, 'How could this happen?' 'Come home, mum,' Hannah said, 'And then set off again.' My holiday was so short it was not worth it and besides, by now a little voice inside me was saying, 'Set off and see!' I had set off once and so I would go ahead and just see.

We parted and I did get a seat on every leg of the journey. Once again God and Charles were working as a team! He rushed home and made lots of phone calls to try and ensure things would be sorted ahead of me. They were, but I did not know he was doing that, so as I arrived at each airport and approached the check-in desk to explain my dilemma, it was God and not Charles who was getting the glory when I found they had managed to squeeze me in somewhere! Looking back I know both deserved thanks, but one more than the other because only one had been responsible for the ticket booking! (Whoops I wasn't going to tell you!)

Why have I recounted this incident? Not to show you that I did set off and see, on the contrary, I set off, but I did not see. I was feeling too stressed and closed into myself and intent on my mission to get to England, whatever. I never really saw, let alone talked to anyone on the journey, until I got to Heathrow and then only superficially because I was tired and was near the end of my journey. When it was time to come back again, I sensed God saying to me, 'OK. Last time you set off, this time I want you to set off and SEE!' And I did. I arrived at Heathrow with a great sense of expectation and excitement. The departure lounge was heaving with people and there were very few spare seats. 'Open your eyes and look.' And I did and then I saw her – a very sad looking young woman sitting alone with one empty seat next to her – I took it. I must have sat there for about twenty minutes while she kept wiping away her tears and I prayed and finally said, 'Do you have a long wait?' That little question led to another and another and for the next hour, before I had to leave to get my flight, she poured out her broken heart to me. She was so like the woman at the well. I was both deeply distressed and exhilarated because I had been able to sit with her, listen to her, hear her and tell her about the 'man of understanding' who she so wanted to meet because she wanted 'more than religion'. We exchanged email addresses as we parted, but we had already made the most important exchange – his offer of life in exchange for her life story. I had been too self absorbed to see anyone on my outgoing journey, maybe there wasn't anyone there, but thank God he didn't disqualify me and I got another chance on the way home. What a gracious God have I!

As we look just one last time at the whole 'Set off and see' principle, I want to end with the place where for me it all started and God taught me through scripture and life's circumstances what a fundamental and freeing lesson this was.

Several years ago I went through a period in my life when I felt what I can only describe as troubled in my spirit. I was restless and in turmoil deep within my heart. During that time God spoke to me through two complete strangers and they both said the same thing. One was a young German mother who I met in transit between Germany and Papua New Guinea. She and her husband had just sold their house, put the contents in storage and were now on their way to be missionaries in that fascinating, far-off land. I asked her about the family, their schooling, all the practical things that a mother's mind immediately thinks of. She could not answer all my questions; she didn't need to. This family was totally confident that the God who was sending them would be with them as they set off into the unknown. 'It's not enough to believe,' she said, 'you have to trust.'

Several days later, I was sitting in a small group at Capernwray Hall, a Bible college in the North of England, where we lived at the time, half listening to a young man from Eastern Europe who was sharing his thoughts on what was going on in his life at the time. His accent was rather thick and I had other things on my mind, but I was thinking how brave he was to be sharing such personal thoughts with a group of strangers and in a foreign language and then I heard it, clear as a bell, that same phrase, 'It's not enough to believe, you have got to trust.' I had got the message! I went and wrote that one potentially life-changing truth in my notebook and continued on in my turmoil, knowing the words were true, but at this point they were not true for me.

Sitting beside a stream, up in the mountains, a few weeks later, I blurted out all my anguish to a friend, finally admitting that my deepest fear and the one that was clouding everything else in my life at that point, was my husband's health. Medically there was no reason to think there was a problem, but in my heart I sensed one and I could keep it to myself no longer. She listened and prayed and I went home and wrote my husband a letter in which I poured out my fear and escalating anxiety. At last I had pinpointed my deepest concern and I admitted it to him writing, 'I think you will have a heart attack and maybe it doesn't have to happen.'

He was kind and gentle in his response, put the letter in his suitcase and went to Canada for two weeks' ministry.

One week later, on a lovely summer evening in June, the phone rang and as I picked it up I heard words that would change our lives for ever, 'Hilary,' the voice said, ' This is John in Canada.' I felt as though I was suddenly suspended in a bubble of silence as I waited for the inevitable and it came, 'Charles is in hospital. He has had a very serious heart attack, but he is still alive.' My legs turned to jelly and my stomach plummeted, but my mind held fast as I asked questions and began to absorb the facts that were coming down the line. He had been out walking. He was miles from anywhere when a truck passed by and finding him sitting on a rock in pain had taken him to the nurses' station. He was now in intensive care. Would I like to speak to the cardiologist? More facts. Medical details. This was a massive heart attack. Charles might not live.

I put the phone down and realised I had to make decisions and make them quickly. I did not wake my son Matthew but brought the girls, Hannah and Laura into the kitchen and, as gently and as clearly as I could, explained the situation to them. They cried and begged me to reassure them that Dad would not die. I could not. ' I do not know,' I said. 'All I know is that God loves us. Do you believe that?' They could not answer immediately, but soon through their sobbing they both bravely said, 'Yes.' 'Then we can trust him,' I said. 'Whatever happens we can trust him. I am not going to pretend to you. If I promised you things that did not turn out to be true you would never believe me again. I don't know what will happen, but God does and we can trust him, so go and start packing. We are going to Canada.'

I made many phone calls and in the midst of all the organising, which had forced me into automatic pilot mode, one of the girls came back into the kitchen. She had been having a talk with God in her room. 'It's going to be OK, I know,' she said. So strong and so sure, she gave me great strength. Now I knew the power of God's presence and the truth of his words so painfully planted in my heart a few weeks before, 'It's not enough to believe, you've got to trust.' I was being forced to 'Set off and see' and what amazing things I saw!

Within the next few hours and days God worked his miracles and I watched in awe! He had gone ahead of us every step of the way. The next morning we had four seats together on a plane, which otherwise was completely full. A Christian flight attendant came to comfort me, during the flight, having noticed how tired I looked. Charles was in the care of one of Toronto's best cardiologists, who had been a friend since childhood. One of my closest friends, in the world, was waiting for me as we got off the plane. We were loved and cared for and helped financially during that long summer in Toronto as we waited for and watched Charles' gradual recovery. God's presence was so real as we stepped into the scenario he had been preparing me for for months. One of the first things Charles said to me when we arrived to find him hanging on to life by a thread and by all the tubes and monitors he was hooked up to, was, 'Are you mad with me?' I could only laugh as I cried!

I would not have chosen this path, but what a precious, painful journey it has been. I set off with fear and trepidation. I had no choice. I set off and I saw God – his love, his care, his tenderness, his complete trustworthiness as we put our trust in him. Each day is still an unknown. We did not know Charles has had heart disease for many years and his heart will therefore always cause concern; each day is just one more opportunity to trust God.

One day I discovered a little group of women who, two thousand years ago, set off on the same journey and discovered the same God doing the most extraordinary things. Their story is found in Mark 16. After their wonderful Jesus had been crucified and buried, they set off expecting to find death, just as I did in my darkest thoughts, but, like me, they found life.

When the Sabbath was over, Mary Magdelene, Mary the mother of James, and Salome bought spices so that they might go andanoint Jesus' body. Very early on the first day of the week, just after sunrise, they were on their way to the tomb and they asked each other, 'Who will roll the stone away from the entrance of the tomb?'

But when they looked up, they saw that the stone, which was very large, had been rolled away. As they entered the tomb, they saw a young man dressed in a white robe sitting on the right side, and they were alarmed.

'Don't be alarmed,' he said. 'You are looking for Jesus the Nazarene, who was crucified. He has risen! He is not here.' (Mk. 16:1-6)

What is so amazing about these women is that they set off with spices to anoint a body, behind a boulder, which was far too heavy for them to move. They could have stayed at home and reasoned this was an impossible mission and it was not worth setting off. But they didn't. They set off, driven by love, asking, 'Who will roll away the stone?' but failing to come up with a reasonable answer. What an adventure! What an opportunity for God to do the impossible and blow aside all their practical reservations. Doubts are no reason not to set off! Take them with you and maybe God will send an angel to silence them! Not only is he ahead of you every step of the way, he is also with you every step of the way, so what are you waiting for?

When I started writing this book I lived in England. During its writing, (somewhere between about chapters 5 and 6!) we moved to Canada. God called us to a wonderful church in Toronto, which just happened to be near Charles' cardiologist and, of course, my good friend. Although it was very clear that we should come and has been for many years (that's another story!) that does not mean it has been easy. Humanly there were many situations and people which could have held us back and prevented us setting off, but we all believe, in our family, that life is an adventure and it was a unanimous decision that we would just 'Set off and see.' We are still in the early days, but there are already many encouragements that God has allowed us to see and we are trusting him that there will be many more.

One Samaritan woman turned a whole town towards Jesus simply because she put down her pot, set off with the living water and gave it away. She did not understand everything, she did not need to. She had got a life and she could not keep it (him) to herself. The days of hiding in the dull, daily routine of existence were over; the adventure was beginning as she stepped into an ancient promise of God which still holds true,

No eye has seen,
No ear has heard,
no mind has conceived
what God as prepared for
those who love him. (Is. 64:4)

Are you willing to take that first tentative step out of the shadows, where you may have lived for so long?

'In him was life, and that life was the light of men. That lights shines in the darkness, but the darkness has not understood it.' (Jn. 1:4–5)

The woman of Samaria did not understand everything. She still stammered in awe, 'Could this be . . .? as she stepped out of the shadows. With her eyes still adjusting to the brilliance of his presence, she set off and made that first move to trust him. She had seen and heard enough to know he was the truth, he was the Messiah, he had found her and he had rescued her.

'He who has the Son has life; he who does not have the Son of God does not have life.' (1 Jn. 5:12)

For the first time in her weary existence, she had got a life.

It's that simple. It's our choice. You want to get a life: simply believe, receive and then hang on for the most amazing adventure which, thanks to Jesus, will go on for ever! You're not sure who he is yet . . . come sit by this well, if you've got half an hour we could talk a while. You tell me your story and then, if you like, I'll tell you mine. Just put your pot down, you can always fill it later, it's not going anywhere. What's that you say, 'Neither are you?' Ever felt like you are stuck in a rut?

McDonald's for the People!

by Richard Wallis

It happened at precisely 9.33 a.m. A massive blow out. After grinding to a halt, it is the silence you notice first. Next you notice the tyre – has it been though an industrial shredding machine? Then the crowd emerge from the village – first the children pulling at the hairs of our arms, followed by the men who gleefully debate our predicament. The women simply wander by with a sideways glance with loads on their heads. For this is not leafy Surbiton but rural central Africa.

Determined that my mission partner, Andrew Stott, and I did not look like a couple of bananas, we sought to give the impression that we were in control. So while our driver joined the debate, we started to quarry stones from along the roadside. When we puffed up the gentle incline with our contribution, the spare tyre was in place and the engine was revving. The driver was keen to get us to our destination – a remote border region. Sometimes, I wonder if the women wandering along that road each day with the loads on their heads look at that pile of stones and smile at the *mzungus* (white men) who played stone castles while their men folk changed a tyre.

I had no idea how far we would travel that day – if I had, I would have insisted at precisely 9.34 a.m. that we returned to the city. The 'hiss' came at 3.29 p.m. A 'hiss' is rarely the harbinger of good news and my great fear is snakes. But there was no doubting this 'hiss' – the hiss of a puncture. We were not stranded at the edge of the world – we were close to the toppling over zone! No second spare tyre; no puncture kit. This time the silence was truly deafening.

We waited on the dirt track for thirty minutes. We prayed. Then we saw the cyclist in the distance taking an eternity to reach us like Omar Sharif on his camel in *Lawrence of Arabia*. But he was cycling east towards the 'toppling over' place – we needed to reach a settlement along the nearest tarmac road, which our driver estimated to be twelve miles due west.

It gets dark in this part of Africa at about 6.30 p.m. Andrew and I decided we would make a dash for it. With a forced march, twelve miles in just less than three hours is not impossible. We prayed again and set off with a purpose. As we swept through a local village with mud huts, at top walking speed in the afternoon heat, we mused if there was a local religion with a prophecy that one day two middle aged *mzungus* would walk right though their village. What did they make of this apparition?

We were down to one small bottle of water between us. We had walked for over an hour and we could now see the horizon – no site of any tarmac road. We encouraged each other. And then we saw our apparition. On the hillside about half a mile ahead was a lorry unloading bricks. Yet we had seen no brick buildings since the morning. But then we understood – all places must have their first brick building and today was the day.

We rushed forward to make sure that the lorry by now approaching from a track to the left would pass us. Being English, we stood in an orderly two-man row and waved our thumbs hitch-hiker style (I know it is pathetic!) The lorry roared past – then braked and immediately stalled. There was space only for Andrew in the cab, so I was hoisted into the back of the open lorry.

The road deteriorated as we moved downhill. Imagine a fast flowing river surging over rocks – we were dry water rafting! After descending, we came to the next village. The children were carrying flags, as this was election week. I was near exhaustion and tried to behave myself. I bit my tongue and remembered my age. But I could not resist the temptation. Since I was a kid, I have longed to be a political candidate and here was my very last opportunity. I had the perfect stage – the back of an open lorry – and I had a crowd of hundreds who could not understand a word I was saying. No point in preaching the gospel. Then I heard the words come out of my mouth, 'McDonald's for the People – vote Richard Wallis!' The crowd cheered. I raised both hands above my head. 'McDonald's today, tomorrow and forever!' The crowd roared. I acted Ronald McDonald and blew kisses to the children. The crowd laughed.

I will never be a political candidate but I think God smiled that day. And he proved again that he remembers his people when they feel they are toppling off the edge of the world – for as dusk came, we discovered that we were more than twelve miles from that tarmac road.

Serving God: Uganda

by Stephen Rand

They had started programmes of care for PWAs – People with AIDS. Which was why that particular morning we had arrived to video a women's group at Kampala Baptist Church, who met in a little prayer chapel by the side of the main building. I was acutely aware that I had never, so far as I knew, ever met anyone with AIDS. I had thought about the theology and the principles, I had been perturbed by the unpleasant and unbiblical judgementalism of some evangelical reactions to the illness – but I had not had to meet anyone facing this particular sentence of death, and in a country which had the barest elements of healthcare available.

As we approached the women round the corner of the church building we could hear them singing: 'God is so good, he's so good to me.' I could scarcely believe my ears. This was one of those moments when I felt a complete pygmy in my faith. These were people whose faith in a loving God was deep and real, or they were most cruelly deluded. I had already learned from John that the church had accepted that their response to those who were HIV positive was not dependent on the reason for their infection. But discovering that some of these women were faithful wives whose legacy from their husbands was to be illness, destitution and early death, made their singing even more remarkable.

For many, the onset of their husband's illness first revealed the reality of his unfaithfulness. It also revealed the possibility that they themselves were infected. Thus they were suddenly precipitated into a maelstrom of emotion and suffering, expected to care for their dying husband in homes with no running water or sanitation, knowing that their husband's death might well leave them homeless, with children to feed and keep in school. Meanwhile they were in an agony of uncertainty about their own condition, with an AIDS test an expensive potential ticket to hopelessness, and every illness perhaps a sign of the end.

These were the people singing of the goodness of God. They gathered for mutual support and encouragement, and to be helped with ideas to generate some income for themselves and their children. As we talked they were sewing a patchwork quilt. One lady backed me to the wall to tell me about her crochet work; or rather, not so much to tell me as to sell me. Her child's education depended on it, she said. She did not need to do much persuading, it seemed the least I could do. I became the proud owner of a set of blue and white woolly table mats. I still have them. They are not much, but they are a reminder of a group of ladies who within two years were no longer with us.

Perhaps not surprisingly they were slightly nervous of the video camera, but when the crew had packed away they asked me about my family. I produced the photos of my daughters I always have with me, and immediately the atmosphere changed and the conversation began to flow. I was asked their names. When I indicated that the older one was called Katharine, one of the younger members of the group became very animated. 'That's my name,' she told me. 'Do you think I could write to your daughter?' I thought this would be fine, and wrote down my address for her. When I arrived home ten days later Katharine had already received her letter; in fact, she wondered why a total stranger could manage to write when her own father did not seem capable.

I asked if I could read it. It was simply stunning.

'I am a born-again Christian and I help with the AIDS ministry of my church. I don't have AIDS but I just wanted to serve God for this time really. I'm on a six months long vacation from junior high school after O-levels, which is ending in June. My brother asked me before the vacation began whether I would like to work with the AIDS ministry. I said, 'Yes, why not?' But inside me I was honestly scared.

Very soon vacation began. The day before I began working I just couldn't settle, till I got on my knees and cried before God. I told him, 'God, listen to this, whatever the case may be, you see I'm quite scared of getting involved with people with AIDS, but I have made up my mind that I'll be a sacrifice to you, O God, with my spirit broken and contrite. I asked the Spirit to empower me to be the best I can to these people.

Right now I'm used to them. I have learned from them and they say they have learned from me. Though there are times which are bad I'm able to cry with them, laugh with them and do things together for the glory of God.'

I have read this out loud in churches many times since, and every time I can feel the tingle on the back of my neck: a Ugandan teenager had discovered more about what it means to follow Jesus than perhaps I ever will.

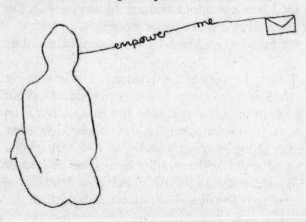

AIDS: The Emergency

by Philip Yancey

As I write this, the rock star Bono, lead singer for the band U2, is travelling across America in a bus, speaking at colleges and churches in an attempt to awaken American Christians to the tragedy of AIDS in Africa. Bono told the students at Wheaton College, 'When 2.5 million people die in Africa each year from AIDS, that's not a cause, it's an emergency . . . There are those who think it will take a miracle [to fix the AIDS problem]. I think it much more likely that God is waiting for us to act. I think he is on his knees begging us to care as he does.'

Counted as Equal? Or Not Counted at All?

by Peter Meadows

Amid the spectacular pageantry of the opening ceremony of the 2002 Commonwealth Games two images captured me. One was of a young adult with Down's Syndrome. The other, a young girl in a wheelchair.

But these were not passive spectators in the crowd, objects of pity, destined to only watch from the stands while much envied able-bodied and able-minded athletes, dancers and 'others' celebrated. In fact, exactly the opposite.

These two were at the very heart of the high-energy celebrations. They were out in the centre of the arena, as part of the exuberant throng. Equal participants, on equal terms. A heart-moving, eye-moistening sight to behold.

And a sound to behold was the Games' International President underlining that these games would be different, because disabled athletes were here on an equal basis. No separate tally of medals for them. Their achievements were to be counted as of equal worth to those of everyone else in their national team.

It marked a significant and ground-breaking change of attitude and it has something to say to those of us concerned about the poor world-wide. Because some estimate as many as one in five of those living in poor communities are disabled.

And though our own attitudes in the west have changed, this is far from a universal experience. A child with a disability is more often seen as an embarrassment to the family, a punishment from God or a burden too heavy to bear. No 'equal terms' for them with supportive government legislation about equal access and equal rights. Instead, they are an object of shame, prejudice, superstition or apathy – paying a high price as a result.

As a far too often result, those who are most in need are hidden from the public eye – by their families or in separate institutions. They become shut out from all that's available to fully able children – including education, social interaction, employment and the dignity of helping their community make a journey out of poverty.

Not untypical is Cho Cho Myaing, who has never left the Burmese (Myanmar) village home where she was born more than thirty years ago. Physically unable to move around, who knows what she could have achieved given the opportunities? Education, marriage, work and the ability to support herself and her family? Instead Myaing has nothing but an uncertain future, while the mother she depends on grows more frail by the day.

For those working with the poor, a hungry child – belly bloated from malnutrition – is hard to miss. But it takes time, commitment and tenacity to identify this hidden face of poverty and to tackle it, including the attitudes at its root.

Yet doing so will mean the difference between life and death, between hope for the future or despair at the years ahead for some of God's most fragile creatures.

Disability in numbers

Behind every one of these statistics is a person

- *There are an estimated 600 million people with disabilities across the globe – one in ten of the world population. Of these, an estimated 120–150 million are children.*
- *World Vision estimates up to one in five of people living in poor communities are disabled.*
- *Research shows violence and abuse are three times more likely to happen to a disabled child.*
- *In Nepal, where marriage is the norm for women, four out of five women with disabilities are reported to be unmarried.*
- *In China, more than half of disabled women over eighteen years old are unmarried.*

List of Contributors

Lord David Alton is an independent cross-bench life peer in the House of Lords and the Professor of Citizenship at John Moores University. The excerpt is taken from *Passion & Pain; The Suffering Church Today* by David Alton with Michele Lombardo, and is available from Jubilee Campaign for £5.99. Tel 01483 894787.

Stuart Briscoe is an international speaker, writer and pastor of Elmbrook Church in Brookfield, USA. He also has a wide TV and radio ministry with his wife, Jill Briscoe. He started preaching at the age of seventeen and served both at Capernwray Bible college and with Torchbearers, an international youth organisation. He has written over forty books.

Compassion exists as an advocate for children: to release them from their spiritual, economic, social and physical poverty, enabling them to become responsible and fulfilled Christian adults. Compassion began its ministry in Korea in 1952. Now, over fifty years on, Compassion works in twenty-two of the world's poorest countries, aiding over 500,000 children through sponsorship.

Keith Danby is the Group Chief Executive of the charity Send the Light Limited in Carlisle. He is the contributing editor for *Stories from Around the World*, Volumes 1 and 2, which have raised over US $200,000 for Christian charities.

Rodney Hui has been a missionary for many years and *Keep Going!* recounts scores of his thoughts and experiences. Invaluable and practical, it is an ideal starter guide to mission as well as being useful to those who are already out there, serving God.

J. John is widely regarded as one of the most creative Christian speakers in the UK. His latest book, *Walking with God* (written with Chris Walley), gives the answers to the big questions in life – what is it all for and is there meaning out there?

Jeff Lucas is one of the UK's most popular speakers and writers, part of the Spring Harvest leadership team, and also a teaching pastor at Timberline church, Colorado. All the extracts from Jeff Lucas in this book were taken from *Lucas on Life* 2, published by Authentic Media.

Peter Meadows is Head of Marketing and Creative Services at World Vision UK. A popular communicator and writer, he co-founded

Spring Harvest and founded Premier Christian Radio. All the extracts written by Pete Meadows come from *Rich Thinking About the World's Poor*, published by Authentic/Spring Harvest publishing division. World Vision can be contacted via their website www.worldvision.org.uk

Sidney Muisyo had been the Communications specialist at Compassion Kenya for the past two years. Before joining Compassion he worked for a marketing PR agency in Nairobi. Sidney works closely with Compassion Kenya's Country Director to implement, advocacy, PR and media relations strategy. He also provides communications material for international partners.

Paul O'Rouke is the President of Compassion Australia. Paul worked as a journalist for many years before joining Compassion Australia's communications department. Four years ago Paul was appointed as President of Compassion Australia, and now leads a committed team from their base in New South Wales.

John Ortberg is a teaching pastor at Willow Creek Community church in Illnois, and writes for Christianity Today and Leadership Journal. All the extracts written by John Ortberg in this book are taken from his book, *If You Want to Walk on Water, You've Got to Get Out of the Boat*, published by Zondervan.

Marcus Oxley is a former country representative for Angola, Concern Worldwide. Concern Worldwide are a Dublin-based organisation who aim to 'enable absolutely poor people to achieve major improvements in their lifestyles which are sustainable without ongoing support'. Concern Worldwide can be contacted on their website, www.concern.ie

Adrian and Bridget Plass sponsor a child through the aid agency, World Vision. Their visit to see her resulted in a book, *Colours of Survival*, from which the chapter was taken from. Adrian is well-known in the UK for his humorous books.

Hilary Price is a popular speaker at a range of events, concentrating mainly on women. Her book, *The Life That Changed My Day*, (Authentic Media) looks at the story of Jesus' meeting with the Samaritan woman and how meeting Jesus can transform a range of life situations. Hilary and her husband Charles now live in Canada, where they lead a large Baptist church.

Stephen Rand is the Co-Chair of Jubilee Debt Campaign, which works for the cancellation of

the unpayable debt of the world's poorest countries. He is also involved in leadership at Kairos Church in Wimbledon. *Guinea Pig for Lunch* recounts the experiences of his travels around the world during twenty-five years working with Tearfund. All the extracts from Stephen Rand in this book come from *Guinea Pig for Lunch*, which is available from Stephen via www.amazon.co.uk

Cherie Rayburn is a freelance writer based in Colorado in the United States. Cherie frequently contributes to Compassion web and print publications. Cherie has travelled widely with Compassion an interviewed many who are directly involved in the ministry overseas.

Janet Root was Senior Communications Specialist for Compassion International. She worked for the organisation for more than ten years as a writer and editor. During her time with Compassion, Janet travelled extensively in the developing world, observing and commenting on Compassion's work from a ground level. Currently, Janet resides in Colorado in the United States and is a freelance writer for World Concern, Mission of Mercy and Compassion International.

Jim Seybert is a Brainstorming and Ideation consultant with the Jim Seybert company.

Emma Stratton started work for Tearfund's Disaster Response Team in 1999 and her assignments included Sudan, Kosovo, Serbia, Jordan and Liberia. She now works part time as a church youth worker and as a freelance coach and trainer. The excerpt comes from her book, *Famines and Facepacks*, published by Authentic/Spring Harvest publishing division. Tearfund can be contacted via their website www.tearfund.org

Viv Thomas has a worldwide preaching and teaching ministry, is a visiting lecturer at All Nations Christian college and an associate professor at Briercrest Seminar in Canada. Ordained as an Elim minister, he started working for OM in 1976 and has been with them ever since, now as an international leadership consultant. His most popular books include *Future Leader* and *Second Choice – Embracing Life as it Is*, both published by Authentic.

Simon Vibert is the vicar of a church in Wimbledon, and Chairman of the Fellowship of Word and Spirit, a publishing organisation and network designed to encourage biblical theology amongst Anglican church leader. The extract cited comes from a forthcoming book on Romans 8 entitled *What in the World Would Make You Want to Give Up?*

Richard Wallis is Head of Missions at Signpost International. He has a passion for serving the poor and you can read about some of his adventures with God in *Stories Around the World 2*. He is a focused person who cannot help laughing at himself.

Tetsunao Yamamori and **Kim-Kwong Chan:** Tetsunao Yamamori is a native of Nagoya, Japan, and President of Food for the Hungry International and visiting professor in the Department of Ethnology at Central University of Nationalities, Beijing, China. Kim-Kwong Chan is Executive Secretary for Education and Training of Hong Kong Christian Council and Visiting Professor in the Department of Philosophy at Hangzhou University, China. Together they wrote *Witnesses to Power*, from which their extract comes. It is published by Authentic Media.

Philip Yancey has written twelve award-winning books, with four selling over a million copies each, including *What's So Amazing About Grace?* He and his wife live in the United States, in Colorado. All his extracts come from his book, *Rumours of Another World*, published by Zondervan. To engage further, visit:
www.RumoursOfAnotherWorld.co.uk